Esther

SEEING GOD WHEN HE IS SILENT

SHELBY TURNER

study suggestions

We believe that the Bible is true, trustworthy, and timeless and that it is vitally important for all believers. These study suggestions are intended to help you more effectively study Scripture as you seek to know and love God through His Word.

SUGGESTED STUDY TOOLS

- A Bible
- A double-spaced, printed copy of the Scripture passages that this study covers. You can use a website like *www.biblegateway.com* to copy the text of a passage and print out a double-spaced copy to be able to mark on easily
- A journal to write notes or prayers
- Pens, colored pencils, and highlighters
- A dictionary to look up unfamiliar words

HOW TO USE THIS STUDY

Begin your study time in prayer. Ask God to reveal Himself to you, to help you understand what you are reading, and to transform you with His Word (Psalm 119:18).

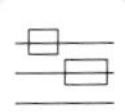

Before you read what is written in each day of the study itself, read the assigned passages of Scripture for that day. Use your double-spaced copy to circle, underline, highlight, draw arrows, and mark in any way you would like to help you dig deeper as you work through a passage.

Read the daily written content provided for the current study day.

Answer the questions that appear at the end of each study day.

The inductive method provides tools for deeper and more intentional Bible study. To study the Bible inductively, work through the steps below after reading background information on the book.

1

OBSERVATION & COMPREHENSION

Key question: What does the text say?

After reading the daily Scripture in its entirety at least once, begin working with smaller portions of the Scripture. Read a passage of Scripture repetitively, and then mark the following items in the text:

- Key or repeated words and ideas
- Key themes
- Transition words (I.e.: therefore, but, because, if/then, likewise, etc.)
- Lists
- Comparisons and contrasts
- Commands
- Unfamiliar words (look these up in a dictionary)
- Questions you have about the text

INTERPRETATION

Key question: What does the text mean?

Once you have annotated the text, work through the following steps to help you interpret its meaning:

- Read the passage in other versions for a better understanding of the text.
- Read cross-references to help interpret Scripture with Scripture.
- Paraphrase or summarize the passage to check for understanding.
- Identify how the text reflects the metanarrative of Scripture, which is the story of creation, fall, redemption, and restoration.
- Read trustworthy commentaries if you need further insight into the meaning of the passage.

3 APPLICATION

Key Question: How should the truth of this passage change me?

Bible study is not merely an intellectual pursuit. The truths about God, ourselves, and the gospel that we discover in Scripture should produce transformation in our hearts and lives. Answer the following questions as you consider what you have learned in your study:

- What attributes of God's character are revealed in the passage?

  Consider places where the text directly states the character of God, as well as how His character is revealed through His words and actions.

- What do I learn about myself in light of who God is?

  Consider how you fall short of God's character, how the text reveals your sin nature, and what it says about your new identity in Christ.

- How should this truth change me?

  A passage of Scripture may contain direct commands telling us what to do or warnings about sins to avoid in order to help us grow in holiness. Other times our application flows out of seeing ourselves in light of God's character. As we pray and reflect on how God is calling us to change in light of His Word, we should be asking questions like, "How should I pray for God to change my heart?" and "What practical steps can I take toward cultivating habits of holiness?"

THE ATTRIBUTES OF GOD

ETERNAL

God has no beginning and no end. He always was, always is, and always will be.

HAB. 1:12 / REV. 1:8 / IS. 41:4

FAITHFUL

God is incapable of anything but fidelity. He is loyally devoted to His plan and purpose.

2 TIM. 2:13 / DEUT. 7:9 HEB. 10:23

GOOD

God is pure; there is no defilement in Him. He is unable to sin, and all He does is good.

GEN. 1:31 / PS. 34:8 / PS. 107:1

GRACIOUS

God is kind, giving us gifts and benefits we do not deserve.

2 KINGS 13:23 / PS. 145:8 IS. 30:18

HOLY

God is undefiled and unable to be in the presence of defilement. He is sacred and set-apart.

REV. 4:8 / LEV. 19:2 / HAB. 1:13

INCOMPREHENSIBLE & TRANSCENDENT

God is high above and beyond human understanding. He is unable to be fully known.

PS. 145:3 / IS. 55:8-9 ROM. 11:33-36

IMMUTABLE

God does not change. He is the same yesterday, today, and tomorrow.

1 SAM. 15:29 / ROM. 11:29 JAMES 1:17

INFINITE

God is limitless. He exhibits all of His attributes perfectly and boundlessly.

ROM. 11:33-36 / IS. 40:28 PS. 147:5

JEALOUS

God is desirous of receiving the praise and affection He rightly deserves.

EX. 20:5 / DEUT. 4:23-24 JOSH. 24:19

JUST

God governs in perfect justice. He acts in accordance with justice. In Him, there is no wrongdoing or dishonesty.

IS. 61:8 / DEUT. 32:4 / PS. 146:7-9

LOVING

God is eternally, enduringly, steadfastly loving and affectionate. He does not forsake or betray His covenant love.

JN. 3:16 / EPH. 2:4-5 / 1 JN. 4:16

MERCIFUL

God is compassionate, withholding from us the wrath that we deserve.

TITUS 3:5 / PS. 25:10
LAM. 3:22-23

OMNIPOTENT

God is all-powerful; His strength is unlimited.

MAT. 19:26 / JOB 42:1-2
JER. 32:27

OMNIPRESENT

God is everywhere; His presence is near and permeating.

PROV. 15:3 / PS. 139:7-10
JER. 23:23-24

OMNISCIENT

God is all-knowing; there is nothing unknown to Him.

PS. 147:4 / I JN. 3:20
HEB. 4:13

PATIENT

God is long-suffering and enduring. He gives ample opportunity for people to turn toward Him.

ROM. 2:4 / 2 PET. 3:9 / PS. 86:15

SELF-EXISTENT

God was not created but exists by His power alone.

PS. 90:1-2 / JN. 1:4 / JN. 5:26

SELF-SUFFICIENT

God has no needs and depends on nothing, but everything depends on God.

IS. 40:28-31 / ACTS 17:24-25
PHIL. 4:19

SOVEREIGN

God governs over all things; He is in complete control.

COL. 1:17 / PS. 24:1-2
1 CHRON. 29:11-12

TRUTHFUL

God is our measurement of what is fact. By Him we are able to discern true and false.

JN. 3:33 / ROM. 1:25 / JN. 14:6

WISE

God is infinitely knowledgeable and is judicious with His knowledge.

IS. 46:9-10 / IS. 55:9 / PROV. 3:19

WRATHFUL

God stands in opposition to all that is evil. He enacts judgment according to His holiness, righteousness, and justice.

PS. 69:24 / JN. 3:36 / ROM. 1:18

TIMELINE OF SCRIPTURE

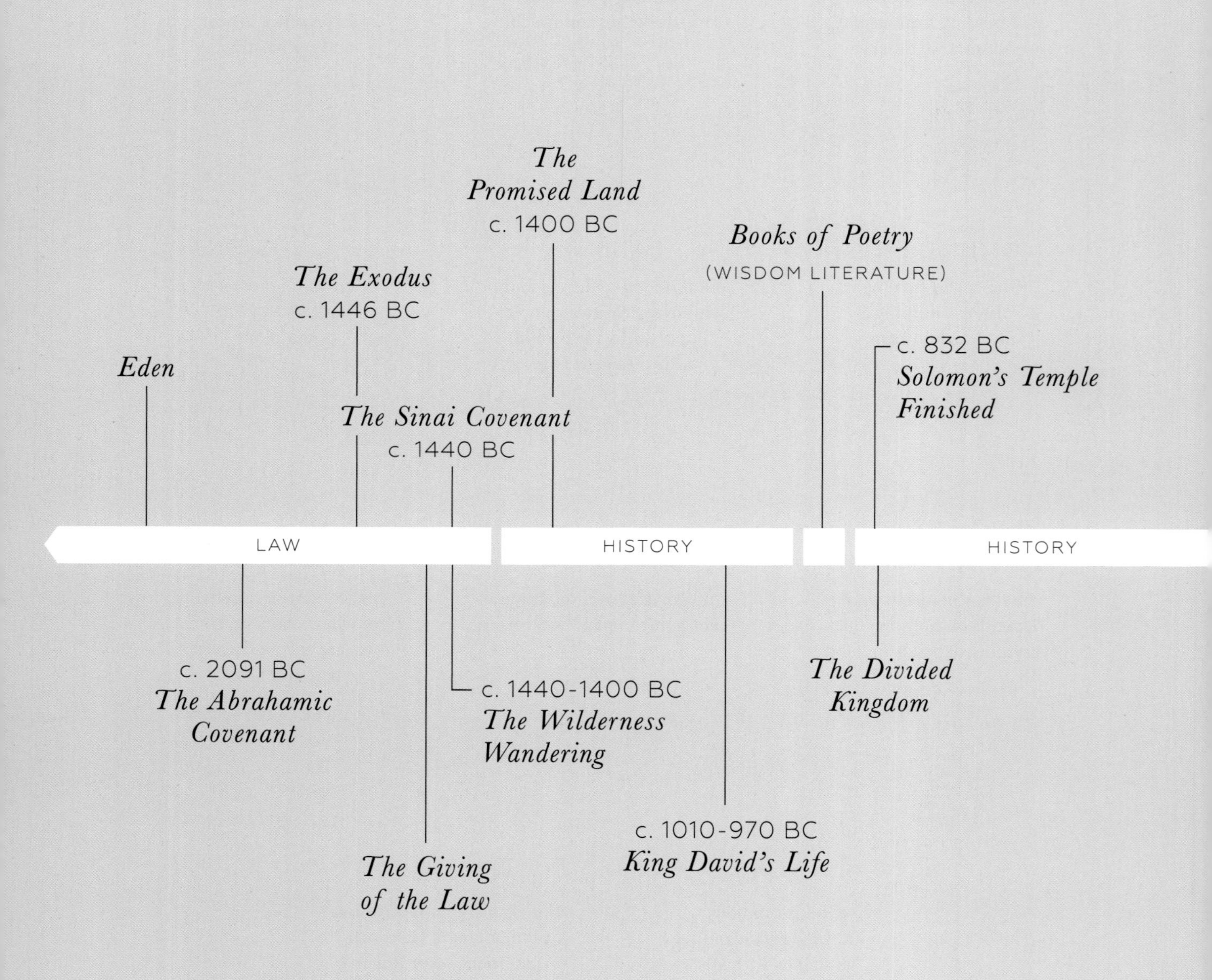

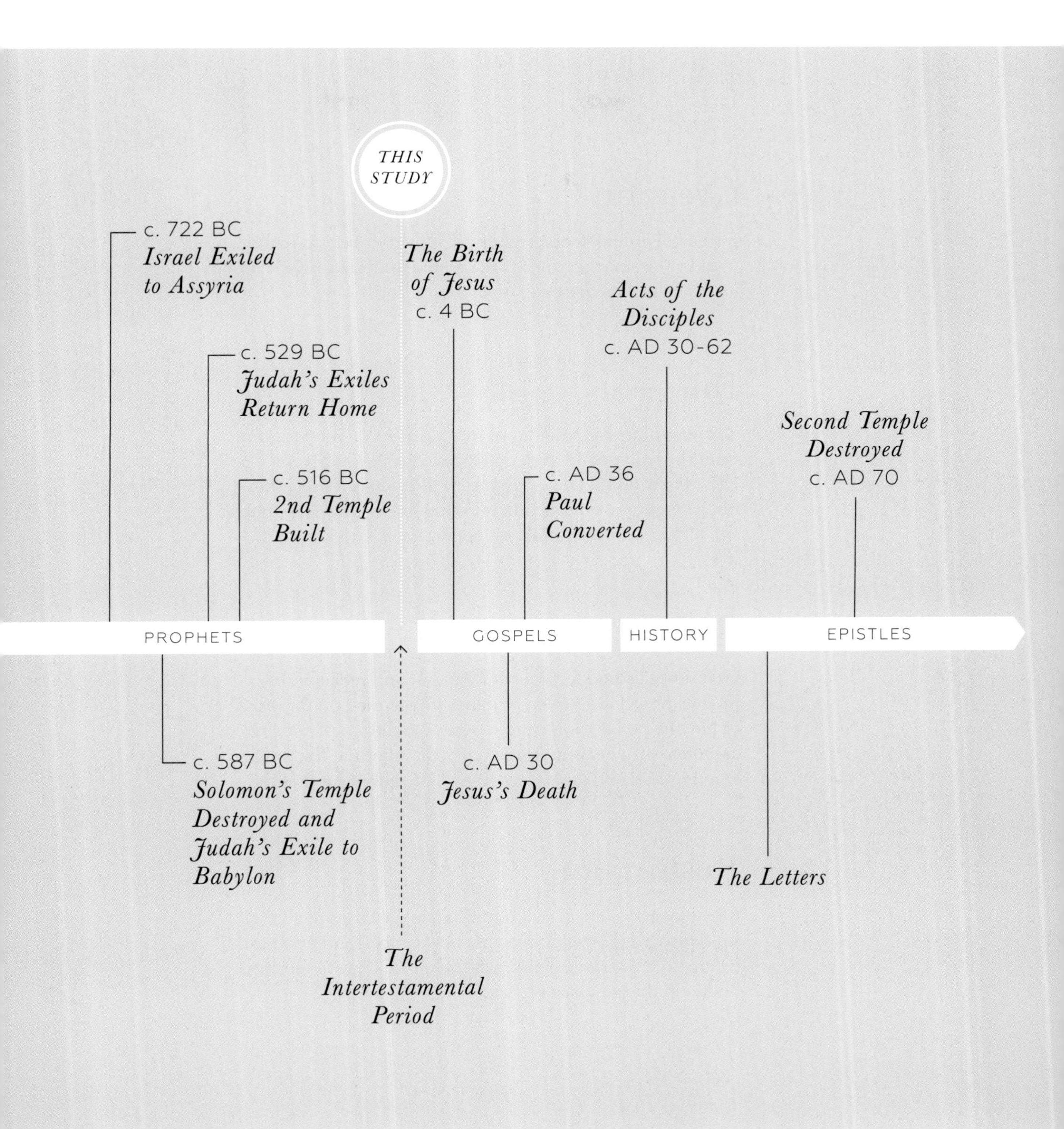

THIS STUDY
c. 722 BC
Israel Exiled to Assyria
c. 529 BC
Judah's Exiles Return Home
c. 516 BC
2nd Temple Built
The Birth of Jesus
c. 4 BC
Acts of the Disciples
c. AD 30-62
c. AD 36
Paul Converted
Second Temple Destroyed
c. AD 70
PROPHETS
GOSPELS
HISTORY
EPISTLES
c. 587 BC
Solomon's Temple Destroyed and Judah's Exile to Babylon
c. AD 30
Jesus's Death
The Letters
The Intertestamental Period

Creation

In the beginning, God created the universe. He made the world and everything in it. He created humans in His own image to be His representatives on the earth.

Fall

The first humans, Adam and Eve, disobeyed God by eating from the fruit of the Tree of Knowledge of Good and Evil. Their disobedience impacted the whole world. The punishment for sin is death, and because of Adam's original sin, all humans are sinful and condemned to death.

Redemption

God sent His Son to become a human and redeem His people. Jesus Christ lived a sinless life but died on the cross to pay the penalty for sin. He resurrected from the dead and ascended into heaven. All who put their faith in Jesus are saved from death and freely receive the gift of eternal life.

Restoration

One day, Jesus Christ will return again and restore all that sin destroyed. He will usher in a new heaven and new earth where all who trust in Him will live eternally with glorified bodies in the presence of God.

ALL OF ESTHER IS A

beautifully illustrated

FORESHADOWING OF THE GOSPEL.

introduction

week one

week two

week three

extras

esther and the canon

Do you know where the Bible came from? If you believe that it came from God, you are undeniably correct. However, instead of dropping it in finished form from the sky, God compiled it over centuries through the pen and paper of ordinary people. Throughout time, educated historians, wise scholars, and faithful followers of God have worked tirelessly to confirm the Bible we hold today is no more and no less than what God intended for it to be. Human hands have been the ones to compile, translate, and validate Scripture, but let us be clear—God is the one and only final authority over His Word. He has no doubts about what should be included in the Bible, and He has, without doubt, preserved its contents fully and completely.

Early church leaders gave the name "canon" to the Bible. This word is derived from the Greek word *kanon* which means "rule" or "standard." For centuries, the Bible had been passed from generation to generation, but there had never been an official list of exactly what writings and books it should include. Many versions of the Bible were universally the same, but a few differed, and those differences were often a point of contention. At the councils of Hippo (AD 393) and Carthage (AD 397), church leaders from around the world ratified the canon, which is the rule and standard of Scripture. The books they included in the canon were verified for accuracy against the oldest available transcripts of the Bible with relentless precision. The ratifying of the canon prevented anyone from either adding to the text or taking away from it. The book of Esther was included in the ratified canon at both of these councils. But this book's acceptance as part of Scripture has not always been so clear-cut.

Unlike every other book of the Bible, Esther never mentions God by name. It takes place in a pagan nation and seems to have a somewhat secular plot. Other books of the Bible, such as Daniel, take place in pagan nations, yet they clearly have divine themes and overt descriptions of God at work. Daniel, for instance, holds fast to his faith and is a witness for God before King Nebuchadnezzar. Esther, though, seems to be just fine living as an unrighteous Persian and has little regard for Jewish laws or the things of God. This has led some scholars to the conclusion that Esther is a secular book that just happens to include the deliverance of God's people, the Jews, and therefore, it has no place in the divinely inspired word of God. Perhaps we can understand where this argument comes from, but the evidence for Esther's inclusion in the canon is much stronger than the argument for its exclusion.

In the earliest available versions of the Hebrew Bible (now called the Old Testament), Esther was included. We do not have an exact date when the Old Testament was first compiled. What we do know is that faithful servants of God wrote down the words of God, and scribes collected, arranged, and preserved these words for centuries—including the story of Esther. This tells us many God-fearing, devoted Jewish scholars believed Esther was not a pagan story but one penned by the hand of God.

Additionally, because the book of Esther was traditionally read at the Feast of Purim and each Jewish family would have had a copy to read in their home, today we have many, many copies of Esther in Hebrew, the original language in which it was written. Among all of the copies of Esther found, some from different factions of Jews living in different regions, there are no glaring differences. This tells us the book of Esther was handled with great care by those who preserved it.

A slight problem occurred when Esther was translated into Aramaic and Greek. Seeking to make the book more holy and less pagan, many additions were added. In fact, in some cases, the book of Esther was made twice as long, including prayers prayed by Mordecai and Esther, as well as other additions to the narrative of the story. This was rectified by many scholars, including Origen (first century AD) and Jerome (fourth century AD), as they compared their Greek and Aramaic versions to the Hebrew originals and saw the major differences. The additions to the book were removed and are not found in standard translations today.

Esther has continually been confirmed as a divinely inspired book and has a secure place in the canon today. By AD 250, there was a nearly universal Old Testament canon, of which Esther was a part. It was confirmed as canonical at the Council of Hippo (AD 393) and Council of Carthage (AD 397). It is universally included as a book of the canon and has been for many centuries. Yet, if any book of the canon could be considered the most controversial in its inclusion, it might be Esther.

Perhaps even the inclusion of Esther in the canon is a precursor to the themes we see in the book itself. Despite questions, concerns, and centuries of translation, Esther has been providentially preserved and remains an integral part of the canon today. Even as men have doubted and distorted it, God has kept it by His hand and for His glory. God is sovereign over all, including every pen stroke in the book of Esther, and we can be sure the book we have today is exactly the book He intended for us to have—no more and no less.

GOD IS SOVEREIGN OVER ALL,
including every pen stroke
IN THE BOOK OF ESTHER.

the persian empire

IN THE TIME OF ESTHER

the historical setting

OF THE BOOK OF ESTHER

TIME	483–474 BC
LOCATION	Susa, the winter residence of the king of Persia
THE CITADEL OF SUSA	The Citadel was the royal compound where the king and all of his attendants and royal officers lived along with his queen, concubines, and harem of women. It was a lavish palace made of the finest materials available. It displayed the tremendous wealth and power of the Persian empire.
JEWS IN SUSA	In 597 BC, the Babylonians captured Judah and brought the Jewish people out of their homes and into Babylonian captivity. This unfortunate tragedy happened not only because of the evil intent of the Babylonian king but also as a consequence delivered by the hand of God to the idolatrous and unfaithful Jewish people (Jeremiah 21). For decades, the Jews lived in suffering and exile, away from home and under the wrath of God.

In 539 BC, Persia conquered Babylon and became the empire in control of the Jewish exiles and their home nation. King Cyrus, the Persian king at the time, was known for being tolerant and understanding of other religious and ethnic backgrounds. He allowed the Jews to return to Jerusalem in 538 BC (Ezra 1:2-3). Although prophets repeatedly called for Jewish people to return to the land the Lord had given them to rebuild the city and the temple, very few returned.

Detailing the triumph and trials of the returned exiles, the books of Ezra and Nehemiah took place within the span of several decades from the events of Esther and help us better understand this portion of redemptive history.

JEWS IN SUSA

Some Jews may have stayed in Persia because they desired to follow God's commands given in Jeremiah 29:6-7: "Find wives for yourselves, and have sons and daughters. Find wives for your sons and give your daughters to men in marriage so that they may bear sons and daughters. Multiply there; do not decrease. Pursue the well-being of the city I have deported you to. Pray to the Lord on its behalf, for when it thrives, you will thrive." But even if this is the reason they stayed, they were ignoring the instructions God gave only a few verses later in Jeremiah 29:10, which states, "For this is what the Lord says: 'When seventy years for Babylon are complete, I will attend to you and will confirm my promise concerning you to restore you to this place.'"

The bottom line is that Jews should not have been in Persia. They were taken there by their disobedience, and in their ignorance, they stayed there after the exile ended. Perhaps they liked the comforts of being part of the richest empire in the known world. Maybe they had assimilated to a Persian way of life and no longer remembered or desired God and His ways. We cannot know what was in their hearts, but we know that Persia was not their home. Yet, God was provident over this unfortunate truth, and out of it, He would work all things according to His redemptive plan and purpose for His covenant people.

AUTHOR

Unknown, possibly Mordecai

PURPOSE

The author wrote Esther to explain the origin of the Feast of Purim.

esther timeline

BEFORE 486 BC
King Darius reigns

486 BC
King Ahasuerus begins reign

AROUND 483 BC
180-Day Feast begins

483 BC
Queen Vashti banished

480 BC
Persian conquest of Greece

479 BC
Persia defeated in Greek conquest

AROUND 478 BC
Search for a new queen

478 BC
Esther crowned queen

Mordecai stopped assassination plot against the king, Haman promoted

474 BC
Haman plots to kill Jews, edict to eradicate the Jews signed, Esther approaches the king, Haman killed, new edict issued that Jews may defend themselves

474 BC (11 MONTHS LATER)
Jews defend themselves and defeat their enemies, Mordecai promoted

473 BC
Ahasuerus reinstates taxes, Mordecai second in command of Persia

465 BC
Death of Ahasuerus and reign of King Artaxerxes I

introduction and themes

READ PSALM 145:14-21, ESTHER 4:13-14, 1 PETER 1:3-5, ROMANS 12:19, COLOSSIANS 1:13-14

What prompted you to pick up this study? Maybe you are unfamiliar with the book of Esther and want to learn what God has to say through this unlikely queen's story. Maybe you know Esther's story includes a moment of brazen bravery, and you are wondering if God is calling you, too, to a bold step of faith. Maybe you are intrigued by how God can work in a book of the Bible that never mentions His name. No matter the reason this study is in front of you, God's Word has much to say to you through these pages.

The plot of Esther rivals the most thrilling Hollywood movie scripts. In it, a carnal king with a hot temper chooses a young orphan as his queen. There are murder plots and genocide threats fueled by centuries-old feuds between rival people groups. There is fear, suspense, bravery, and justice. Not one moment of this book is trivial or mundane.

Throughout this study, we will unpack every piece of Esther's story with historical accuracy and careful consideration of how God worked in it. The book of Esther will open your eyes to see how God is always active, always committed to His redemptive plan, and always the hero of the story—even when the story does not mention His name.

As we walk together through the book of Esther, there are a few themes to watch for. Let us take an in-depth look at each one, so we can identify them when they arise.

DIVINE PROVIDENCE – PSALM 145:14-21

Providence is a difficult concept to grasp, and current cultural ideas such as karma or fate often impact our view of it. But providence in the Bible is not the work of chance, luck, or so-called mystic forces of the universe. Rather, it is the work of God as He provides for our needs in His sovereign timing.

Divine providence is God's preplanned, willful, and personal response to the needs of humanity.

This kind of provision is on display throughout Esther. We may not see a flashing neon sign saying, "God's providence is at work here!" However, we know divine providence is always at work.

HUMAN BRAVERY – ESTHER 4:13-14

Esther and Mordecai's bravery may be the most well-known theme of this book. You cannot deny that King Ahasuerus was reckless and maniacal at times, and Esther risked her life by standing in his presence uninvited. Esther's courage is admirable, but it does not make her the hero of this story. God is the hero, working through Esther to do the impossible.

We will see that Esther's true bravery is her courage to obey the Lord, and that is the courage we should emulate. Her story will encourage us to examine where God has placed us and consider how He is asking us to participate in His plan, right where we are.

THE PERISHING EMPIRES OF MEN AND THE IMPERISHABLE KINGDOM OF GOD – 1 PETER 1:3-5

One of the great ironies of this book is that the most powerful king of the most powerful nation is repeatedly bested. His wife publicly humiliates him, he loses a war, he sends senseless edicts at the request of his advisers, and he moves at the whim of his new queen, Esther.

This is not a statement about the weakness of a powerful man so much as it is an illustration of the weakness of the empires men build. No man is fit to reign over the earth. No empire he can build will fulfill all his desires.

There is another kingdom represented in Esther's story—the kingdom of God. This kingdom is ruled by a just and loving King who protects His people with His power. Everything He wills comes to pass. His kingdom never perishes. And He presides over all men and their empires with infinite power, using them to show His glory.

Throughout this study, pay close attention to the empire of Persia and the kingdom of God. One will crumble, and one will remain forever.

GOD'S RESPONSE TO HUMAN EVIL – ROMANS 12:19

Evil is on display in the book of Esther. The Persian empire was filled with sinful practices and people. One of the most evil people in the book is Haman. Haman has a deep-seated hatred for God and His people, the Jews, and Mordecai in particular. In Haman's pride, he seeks to arrange praise for himself and demise for Mordecai. But Haman's life is a study in the way God providentially executes justice. God's providence delivers the fate Haman deserves.

FORESHADOWING OF THE GOSPEL – COLOSSIANS 1:13-14

The final theme to watch for is the gospel. The gospel is the very good message that Jesus has come to earth and given His life as payment for the sins of all mankind. The Bible tells us the punishment for sin is death, but Jesus's death satisfied the required payment for sin before God for all who believe.

How can we see the gospel in a book written before Jesus was born? One beauty of Scripture is that it all points toward Jesus. The gospel is foreshadowed in many ways through Esther. As Jews, Esther and Mordecai are part of God's chosen people, through whom He has promised to bring a Messiah. Even though Esther and Mordecai are imperfect, God saves the entire Jewish population through them. God is a God who keeps His promises, and in this story, He protects His covenant people. One day, He would send the Messiah to provide eternal protection from death for all who believe.

God's providence in Esther's story provides temporary peace for God's people. In His life, death, and resurrection, Jesus provides eternal peace for all who believe in Him. Esther is a glimpse at the overarching theme of Scripture—that God has made a way for all mankind to live in the safety and security of His presence for eternity in Jesus.

IN HIS LIFE, DEATH, AND RESURRECTION,

Jesus provides eternal peace

FOR ALL WHO BELIEVE IN HIM.

Describe God's providence as seen in Psalm 145:14-21.

Read Deuteronomy 31:6. What reason does God give to be courageous in this verse? What does this mean for how you are to be courageous in your own life?

Read Romans 12:17-21. What is God's role in executing justice to our enemies? What is our role?

Write a prayer asking God to reveal Himself and the way He is always providentially working to you through this study.

themes in esther

DIVINE PROVIDENCE	God's response to the needs of man is preplanned, willful, and personal.
HUMAN BRAVERY	This bravery is acting with God-given courage, even when it leads to the risk of personal harm.
THE PERISHING EMPIRES OF MEN & THE IMPERISHABLE KINGDOM OF GOD	Every earthly empire built by men is ultimately used by God for His glory.
GOD'S RESPONSE TO HUMAN EVIL	God is sovereign over human evil, and He delivers just consequences to evildoers, both on earth and in eternity.
FORESHADOWING OF THE GOSPEL	Through Jesus, God has made a way for all mankind to live in the safety and security of His presence for all eternity.

WEEK ONE — DAY TWO

the fall of queen vashti

READ ESTHER 1

Esther's story begins not with her but with another Persian queen named Vashti. Vashti's name means "the best, desired, and beloved." While King Ahasuerus of Persia had hundreds of wives, he only had one queen. We can infer that Vashti was his favorite wife, a prized possession of a powerful king.

We learn that King Ahasuerus, whose name is sometimes translated as "King Xerxes" by different Bible translations, governs a kingdom that extends from India to Cush, which was most of the known world at this time. Ahasuerus is certainly a man of great influence, and in the year 483 BC, he threw an opulent party to prove it. This party, which lasted about six months, was thrown for one purpose—to display the glorious wealth and magnificent splendor of his kingdom (Esther 1:4).

The concluding week of the party was the grand finale. All, from the least to the greatest within the citadel of Susa, were invited to eat, drink, and enjoy the pleasures of the kingdom. And they did. In verse 8, we are given an idea of how Ahasuerus wielded his power. It says that according to the royal decree, there were no restrictions on drinking; everyone was allowed to drink whatever they wanted. During this time period, it was typical to say that in the presence of the king, no one could drink unless the king drank, and when the king drank, all in his presence must also drink. Lifting this rule for the grand finale perhaps reveals that the only thing Ahasuerus liked more than being in control was throwing a lavish party.

On the last day of the party, when he was "feeling good from the wine," Ahasuerus demanded his queen, Vashti, appear before his party goers (who were all male as the women had a separate party). He ordered Vashti to appear so they could gaze at her beauty. He asked her to wear her royal crown when she came. It is unclear if he intended for her to wear anything else or not. He had been strutting his strength and power for 180 days, and now, he wanted to show off his most prized possession—his wife. We do not know the nature of Ahasuerus's relationship with Vashti, but given what we know of his character so far, it is not hard to imagine the way he treated her. It is likely that, to him, she was simply a feast for his eyes, his personal servant for his most intimate needs, just another kingly conquest.

The irony of what happens next cannot be overstated. At the end of his over-the-top display of wealth, where he wanted everyone to fawn at his greatness, his own wife refuses to yield to his power. She declines to come at his beckon. The author gives no reason why she did this. We could imply endless scenarios that led to her refusal, but all we really know is that she would not come. And the king was angry.

Ahasuerus, fueled by his anger, decides his pride is on the line, and he must stop others from exercising such shameful rebellion against him. Vashti must be publicly punished. He pulls together his closest advisers and asks what should be done. They agree Vashti shall never enter the king's presence again, and she will be replaced by another, better queen. This is a curious consequence as it gave Vashti what she wanted: to be nowhere near the king. Ahasuerus and his advisers also decide an edict will be sent to every household in the far-reaching Persian empire, decreeing men should be the masters of their house and women were to submit to their mastery.

As we will see throughout Esther, Ahasuerus is greatly overreacting by sending this edict. He is bringing the entire nation into a spat between him and his wife. He is grasping for command of his empire, easing his bruised ego, and relying on bad advice from drunken friends.

At this point in the story, Ahasuerus is losing his battle for control. God, however, is not. While Ahasuerus's actions seem reckless and Vashti's rebellion against him seems a small detail when the king had hundreds of other wives, God was providentially moving in all of this. He is putting everything in place to make Esther queen, so she can execute His plan and show His power and glory.

It is important to stop here and note that, not unlike Ahasuerus, we love to build empires of our own. We love for people to marvel at them. But at this moment, the most powerful man in the world, after displaying his unmatched wealth, is humbled by just one refusal from his wife. Worldly empires are never as impressive as they seem. There is only one kingdom that is imperishable, and that is the kingdom of God. The actions of Ahasuerus make us long for a better King, a King who is truly powerful and uses His power for ultimate good.

Ahasuerus was vengeful, yet Jesus is merciful.

Ahasuerus demanded, yet Jesus sacrificially loves.

Ahasuerus was not worthy of honor, yet Jesus is worthy of all our honor and praise.

Jesus is the Savior, the Light of the World, the slain and risen Lamb of God. He is everything we need and all we desire in a king. He is worthy of our obedience, and we should come when He calls us, knowing that all He asks us to do is for our good and His glory (Romans 8:28).

THERE IS ONLY ONE KINGDOM THAT IS IMPERISHABLE, AND THAT IS *the kingdom of God.*

Describe what you think King Ahasuerus may have been like based on today's Scripture reading.

Read Romans 8:28. How do you think God will use Vashti's refusal and the king's reckless actions to fulfill His plans for the Jewish people? How might God use difficult circumstances in your life for your good and His glory?

Read Revelation 21:1-8. Describe King Jesus.

How does Jesus differ from the kings of this world?

WEEK ONE — DAY THREE

the rise of esther

READ ESTHER 2:1-18

The young often pen a hopeful story of how their future will unfold. In these wishfully written tales, they experience meaningful relationships, success, and a life full of joy and comfort. Yet, these stories hardly ever turn out as envisioned. This does not mean that life is any less lovely, but it does mean the beauty of life is hidden beneath layers of heartache and hardship. Our leading lady, Esther, is a prime example of this reality.

As chapter 2 begins, Esther is introduced as three things: an orphan, a Jew, and a woman of striking beauty. Esther's caring cousin, Mordecai, had become her guardian, and although they were Jewish by descent, they lived in pagan Persia. Their relatives had been exiled from Jerusalem by the Babylonians. Years later, the Persians defeated the Babylonians and gained control over Jerusalem and the rest of the Babylonian empire. At this time, the Persian king allowed Jews to return to Jerusalem if they so desired.

God's spokespeople, the prophets, encouraged Jews to return to their home city where they could freely worship the Lord, but Mordecai and Esther's relatives chose not to return. We do not know why this Jewish family chose to stay in Susa. We do know Jews were considered outsiders and undesirables in Persia, much like they were under Babylonian rule. It was not favorable to be Jewish, one of God's chosen people, probably because the Persian culture was woefully opposed to living according to God's commands. Why does this matter? It matters because Esther is about to be thrust from her obscure life as an orphaned Jewish girl to the center of Persian opulence in the king's palace.

Some scholars believe the second chapter of Esther takes place as long as four years after the first. During that time, Ahasuerus has tried his hand at conquesting Greece and lost. In his defeat, he remembers another humiliating blow he suffered at the hands of Vashti when she refused him. His advisers, seeing his melancholy, suggest he should search for a new and better queen. But their plan to go about this task is sinister. They will round up every beautiful virgin in all of Persia and bring them to the king. He will be given one night with each woman to determine her beauty and worth, and then he can choose the one he likes best to be crowned as his new queen.

To be crowned queen was not a fairytale story of rags to riches. It was not a beauty contest that any woman wanted to win. This royal competition of virgins was exactly as demeaning as you are imagining. And once a woman had spent a night with the king, she was his property for life. She could not marry another or even leave the harem. She would grow old in seclusion as a concubine unless the king chose her as queen.

The nationwide search for lovely women gets underway, and it is no surprise that Esther is taken to the palace. Immediately, she earns the favor of the eunuch, Hegai, in charge of the women. It is worth mentioning here that the Persian empire was as ruthless to men as it was to women. Women were taken to please the king. Men were taken and castrated to attend to the king's hundreds (if not thousands) of women. These castrated men were called eunuchs. No one was safe from empiric control.

Esther received months of beautification treatments. She needed to be transformed from a commoner to a potential royal, after all. During this time, Mordecai, likely concerned for Esther's well-being, checked on her daily. And Esther, under his direction, kept her identity as a Jew a strict secret.

Then it was finally Esther's turn to go to the king for a night. We cannot know what Esther felt at this moment, but we can attempt to put ourselves in her shoes. She is expected to please the king physically and emotionally to gain his favor and win the crown of the queen. It is doubtful whether or not she even wanted to "win" this contest of sorts.

As a Jew, she likely knew intimacy with a man before marriage was forbidden. She knew a lot of the things in which she was partaking were forbidden—the clothes she wore, the food she ate, the culture she was forced to embrace. But she had little choice. Was she breaking the Jewish Levitical law? Yes. Would God take His providential hand from her because of this? No, He surely would not. God is the hero, and He is always faithful.

Esther's night comes and goes, and the king concludes he loves her most. The word "love" used in verse 17 translates much more like "excited lust" than "tender affection," but regardless, Esther is crowned queen. King Ahasuerus and the nation rejoice that he has found what he wanted in a queen. However, the people fail to realize one thing. Even though Ahasuerus chose Esther, she was ultimately chosen by God.

God placed Esther in Susa rather than back in Jerusalem where one could argue she better belonged. God formed Esther to be lovely in form and feature. God granted her favor with all the people she encountered, including the king. God chose the Jewish people as the ones from which His Son would enter the world as Savior. And as we will see, God will be intricately involved in the preservation and deliverance of these people for the sake of His name and glory.

Ahasuerus believed he had power. Mordecai believed Esther would be safe from this power if her Jewish identity was unknown. Esther believed she had been crowned a servant of the king. But, truly, God alone is the One in control, and we will see this play out as the story unfolds.

In our own lives, God's power is equally potent. He controls every detail, and we can trust that in all things, He is working to bring His plans and purposes to pass.

God alone is the One in control,

AND WE WILL SEE THIS PLAY OUT

AS THE STORY UNFOLDS.

Esther 2:5 tells us Mordecai is a descendant of a man named Kish. Read 1 Samuel 9:1, 1 Samuel 10:1, 17-23. Who was Kish in this verse? Who was his son?

What do you think it was like to be a Jew living in Persia? How do you think this might compare to being a Christian living in today's secular world?

How have you seen the providence of God in the book of Esther so far? What does this tell you about how God is providentially working in your life?

Read Genesis 50:20. God does not always save His people from experiencing evil, but He does always use it for good. Where do you see this in Esther's story? What could this mean for your own story?

human dignity in esther

In the first two chapters of Esther, we have repeatedly witnessed the Persian empire's unfortunate degradation of people. Everyone in the empire was subject to the power of the king. Whatever he commanded came to pass. It is unlikely that anyone attempted to evade or disobey his orders for fear that if they did, they would receive a harsher sentence still. This reality of life in ancient Persia is not something we can avoid while reading and studying the book of Esther. We have seen Esther taken from her home, women used and discarded by the king, men castrated and ripped of their futures, and there will be more evil to come. What do we do with the troublesome way the Persian empire refused to acknowledge human dignity? We process it in light of what we know about God and His Word.

THE BIBLE IS OFTEN DESCRIPTIVE NOT PRESCRIPTIVE.

Throughout the entire Bible, we see vile practices described and horrific stories play out. However, just because these things are in the Bible does not mean God condones them. In fact, often the exact opposite is true. Evil is often mentioned in the Bible in order to condemn it, even if that is not explicitly stated. When evil is described, that does not mean it is being prescribed as an acceptable way to live. The Persian empire's treatment of people was not acceptable to God.

WE LOOK TO JESUS ALONE AS OUR EXAMPLE.

Even the kindest humans will fail to treat others with dignity and respect at times. The only one who can teach us how to care for others as God intended is God Himself made flesh—Jesus. Jesus's example is different from the Persian empire in every way.

PERSIAN EMPIRE	JESUS
Authoritarian control	Servant leadership (Matthew 20:28)
Flippant	Wise (Isaiah 11:2)
Self-centered	Submitted to God's will (John 5:19)
Self-gratifying	God-glorifying (Philippians 2:11)
Inconsiderate of others	Perfectly cares for the needs of others (Matthew 6:30)
Steals, kills, destroys	Offers abundant life (John 10:10)
Demands others sacrifice their lives for their good	Sacrificed His life for the good of all (Hebrews 7:27)
Prideful	Humble (Matthew 11:29)

mordecai's intervention

READ ESTHER 2:19-23

The plot of Esther has already taken us on a wild journey. Just when it seems there is calm to be found now that the search for a new queen has concluded, another plot twist arises. After Esther's celebratory banquet, for some reason, there was another gathering of the virgins. Perhaps Ahasuerus's appetite for young women was not fulfilled in Queen Esther, and so he wanted to add to his harem of concubines. This is not a far-fetched idea considering Ahasuerus's temperament and cultural norms at the time. Whatever the reason, they gathered, and at that time, Mordecai was sitting at the king's gate. Now, this is significant. Not just anyone can sit at the king's gate; you must have a royal position to be seated here. This implies that Mordecai was employed as a civil servant of the empire in some way. Most likely, this status allowed him access to Esther he otherwise would not have had.

Mordecai's position also provided him access to a conversation between Bigthan and Teresh, two of the king's eunuchs. They were plotting to assassinate the king. It is not hard to imagine what fueled these men to hate the king so much that they wanted to see his demise. He had most likely taken them from their families and destroyed their lives. And assassination plots were common in ancient Persia. In fact, in 465 BC, Ahasuerus will be killed in a successful assassination attempt. But this one was not successful, thanks to Mordecai.

When Mordecai overhears the plot against the king, he brings it to Queen Esther. One can only imagine the moral dilemma he faced at that moment. It is unlikely that he had much respect for the king. After all, he was the man who had taken his cousin and made her his wife with no regard for her consent. And the king was rash, angry, and prideful. But even if Mordecai did not respect him, he did seem to fear him. And perhaps he thought saving the king's life would win his favor toward Esther and himself. Whatever his thought process, however he wrestled with what to do with this dismal information, he chose to share it. And Esther shared it with the king. The matter was investigated and verified, and the men were hanged on the gallows, which probably meant they were impaled on large, wooden poles. We can only wonder what Mordecai and Esther felt when these men were killed. Did they feel partly responsible? Who can know? They saved the life of one man, and two were killed in his place.

Over and over again in Esther, we see Mordecai and Esther—who are Jews, the chosen people of God, commanded to keep the law of Moses—put in very difficult moral situations. Should Esther sleep with the king? Should she reveal or conceal her identity? Should Mordecai snitch on the sinister plans so that he may save an evil king? It is tempting to moralize or demoralize their actions. But we simply cannot do that. The author does not do this, so neither should we. What we can do is continually look for the way God providentially works through each and every word and action to cause His plan and purpose to come to pass.

Do you think it was an accident that Mordecai overheard the two men plotting? No, it was no accident. Yet this is one of the many sequential dominoes in the providential plan of God in Esther. And the next domino is an unlikely one.

Persian kings were known for their reward of good, loyal behavior. It is well documented in history that they had official lists of "King's Benefactors" in their royal archives. Yet, Mordecai, who saves the life of the king, is not rewarded at all—at least in this moment. This, too, was not due simply to oversight but to the hand of God. We will see why a little later.

What can we learn from today's study? We can consider verses like Galatians 6:10 and Romans 12:14-20 that tell us our duties as Christians are to do good to all, as far as it depends on us. We can remember that in the stickiest of moral situations, where we must pick between bad and worse, we have the wisdom of God's Word and the leading of the Holy Spirit to help us. But we also have a God who is not far off but right there with us.

God is active in injustice, in brokenness, in desolation. God works through the wrong and wicked things of this world to bring about His good and perfect plans. God did this for Esther and Mordecai, and He will do this for all those who believe in Him.

And finally, the records of King Ahasuerus remind us to look to King Jesus, who also keeps records. Only, His records are not just of what we have done for Him but also what He has done for us. And unlike the carnal king in Esther, what King Jesus does for us outweighs anything we could ever do for Him. Those who believe in Christ are eternally secure because He shed His blood to cover their sins. They are saved by grace alone, through faith alone. The kingdom of God is better than the empire of Persia, and Jesus is the true and better King.

THOSE WHO BELIEVE IN CHRIST
ARE ETERNALLY SECURE BECAUSE
He shed His blood to cover their sins.

List all the places you see the providence of God on display in Esther 2:19-23.

Read John 14:15-17, 26. What is the Holy Spirit's role in the life of a Christian according to these verses? What impact does this have on Christians when they face difficult decisions?

Read Galatians 6:7-10. What do these verses mean for how we live our day-to-day lives?

Read Revelation 20:11-15 and Ephesians 2:1-9. Who is judged by their works? What role does the book of life play? How does one get their name written in the book of life?

haman's plot against the jews

READ ESTHER 3:1-15

Five years have passed since Esther was crowned queen. It is important to note the passage of time because Esther can seem like a very fast-paced book, with God making big, visible moves left and right. But in reality, Esther took place over a period of about ten years. Many of Esther's and Mordecai's days were just like any other. Though not every day was worth mentioned in Scripture, God was still active and moving. Every day is a day when God is at work.

Today's Scripture reading, though, is packed with life-altering action. As chapter 2 begins, we meet a new character, Haman, who has been promoted to the highest position of all the officials in Persia. But maybe more important than his position is his identity. Haman is the son of Hammedatha the Agagite, and the Agagites have a long history with the Jews. Haman was a descendant of King Agag, who we see in 1 Samuel 15:8-9. King Agag was an Amalekite, a people group completely and utterly opposed to God and His people. Therefore, God told the Israelites to kill them all. Yet, King Saul did not. He left King Agag alive. The prophet Samuel later killed King Agag when he realized Saul did not follow the Lord's instructions.

The Amalekites and the descendants of King Agag, as a whole, did not simply dislike Jews; they were pawns in the hands of the serpent found in the garden of Eden. In Genesis 3, the serpent deceived Eve and Adam, and sin entered the world through their disobedience to God. In Genesis 3:15, God declares there will be enmity between the woman's offspring (all those who believe in Jesus and are saved) and the serpent (who is the tempter, Satan). The Agagites were the visible fruition of that enmity. They hated God and His people, the Jews, with an otherworldly passion. With this in view, we can see how the following scene escalated so quickly.

As the newly promoted Haman walks through Susa, the people are instructed to bow in honor. This was not a bow in worship; it was just a customary way to honor someone in authority. Think of it like a head nod or tip of the hat. Mordecai, who never seems to have protested bowing to the king, refuses to bow to Haman. When Haman hears of this, he is "filled with rage." Then, he learns of Mordecai's ethnic identity. He is a Jew. Haman's rage turns otherworldly, fueled by pure evil. At that moment, Haman planned to destroy every

Jew in the empire. He determined to convince King Ahasuerus to let it happen.

Haman approaches the king and gives a vague description of a rebellious people group. The king hardly seems to care and agrees to the genocide with shocking ease. Maybe it was the large sum of silver Haman promised in exchange for permission to carry out this plan. Maybe it was the fact that the king valued no one's life but his own. Whatever the reason, he gave his signet ring to Haman. The signet ring was used to stamp the king's approval on edicts. By handing the ring to Haman, Ahasuerus effectively says, "Let it be so."

Haman, evil brimming from every pore of his body, summons all who were necessary to write this preliminary plan into an irrevocable edict. Where is God's providence in this moment? It is woven into every tiny detail, as we will see in the coming weeks, but it is especially present in Esther 3:7. Before Haman brought this plan to King Ahasuerus, he used a pur, which was like a die, to determine what would be the best possible day to exterminate the Jews. He threw the pur. It rattled, rolled, and fell on the month of Adar, the twelfth month of the year. With his plot hatched in the first month of the year, Haman believed this timeline was determined by fate. But Proverbs 16:33 teaches the opposite, saying, "The lot is cast into the lap, but its every decision is from the Lord."

The day Haman cast the pur to determine the fate of the Jews just so happened to be in the month the Jews celebrate Passover. Passover commemorated a time in their history when death swept over Egypt, killing every firstborn of every home, except the homes that had the blood of a lamb painted around their door frame. Every Jewish home marked with the blood of the slain lamb was spared from death. And now, hundreds of years later, another edict of death on nearly the same date was set into motion. Would God again spare His people from death?

As we end this chapter, couriers are riding forth, delivering the grim edict to every city and province in the Persian empire. Haman and King Ahasuerus are celebrating with a glad drink. The city of Susa is overcome with confusion, and the Jews were likely in total despair. But God? This was always His plan. He knew, as indicated in Genesis 3:15, that the empire of the world would be in constant pursuit to destroy His people. His people would surely feel the effects of sin, evil, and the dark schemes of the serpent. Yet, one day Jesus would come, deliver the final blow to the serpent, and redeem all of God's people. Until He arrives, the people of God will be preserved by God and for God. Haman thought he had the upper hand, but God always has the final say.

The providence of the Lord reigns, even here in the lowest point of the story for God's people. We can trust that we who have believed in Christ are also God's people, and the same is true for us. At our lowest, God's plan remains unchanged. He will accomplish all He has set forth to do. Nothing can stop His redemption of the world—or of us as believers—through Jesus. Nothing.

The providence of the Lord reigns,

EVEN HERE IN THE LOWEST POINT OF THE STORY FOR GOD'S PEOPLE.

Read Genesis 12:2-3 and 1 Samuel 15:2. Why are these verses significant? What do they say about the Amalekites and Agagites? What do they say about Haman?

Read Exodus 12:1-18. Describe God's protection of His people in these verses. What is the significance of Haman's plot being set in motion the day before the Jews commemorated the Passover?

Read Psalm 2. How does this chapter put Haman's opposition to the Jews into perspective? How might this apply to the opposition you personally face for your faith?

Take a moment to stop and pray the Lord's prayer found in Matthew 6:9-13. What phrases in this prayer speak to the spiritual opposition Christians face?

biblical timeline

The Amalekites attack the Israelites at Rephidim shortly after their exodus from Egypt.

EXODUS 17:8-16

God reminds the Israelites of the attack of the Amalekites who do not fear Him. He commands the Israelites to destroy the Amalekites when they enter the Promised Land.

DEUTERONOMY 25:17-19

God commands King Saul to destroy all of the Amalekites in retribution for their attack on Israel. Saul destroys all of the Amalekites but one, King Agag. The prophet Samuel kills King Agag. Some of the Amalekites likely escape Saul's conquest as they appear again later in history.

1 SAMUEL 15:1-35

The Amalekites plunder David's camp and steal their wives and children. In response, David destroys all of the Amalekites he can. Four hundred Amalekite men escaped.

1 SAMUEL 30:1-31

The sons of Simeon of Judah strike down a remnant of the Amalekites who lived at Mount Seir.

1 CHRONICLES 4:43

Haman the Agagite, descendant of the Amalekites, plots to kill all of the Jews in Persia.

ESTHER 3:1-10

Haman and those who sought to kill the Jews are destroyed, and the Jews are preserved.

ESTHER 7:1-10, 9:1-16

WEEK ONE — DAY SIX

THE LORD IS RIGHTEOUS IN
ALL HIS WAYS AND FAITHFUL
IN ALL HIS ACTS.

psalm 145:17

Week one reflection

REVIEW ESTHER 1-3

Paraphrase the passage from this week.

What did you observe from this week's text about God and His character?

What does this week's passage reveal about the condition of mankind and yourself?

How does this passage point to the gospel?

How should you respond to this passage? What specific action steps can you take this week to apply this passage?

Write a prayer in response to your study of God's Word. *Adore God for who He is, confess sins that He revealed in your own life, ask Him to empower you to walk in obedience, and pray for anyone who comes to mind as you study.*

WEEK TWO — DAY ONE

a plan to save the jews

READ ESTHER 4

When we left off, an edict had been sent out condemning the Jews to death on the thirteenth day of the twelfth month. There was confusion among the residents of Susa and celebration at the palace. And this dichotomy is exactly where we pick up in chapter 4 as the story narrows to focus on Mordecai and Esther.

Mordecai has likely realized that his refusal to bow to Haman has led to total and utter destruction. All Jews are now facing the sword and spear because he refused to lower himself in honor of Haman the Agagite. Mordecai weeps in sackcloth and ashes as all of the Jews in Persia wail with him. However, one Jew is not yet burdened by this news.

Esther seems to have no idea this plot has been put into place because she sends Mordecai some fresh clothes and says effectively, "Cheer up, cousin!" Mordecai is not uplifted by her gift. Confused, she sends a letter asking him why his sadness is so deep. He replies with an explanation of the situation and a copy of the edict. At the end of his explanation, he also includes a command—Esther must be the one to ask the king to stop the impending terror against the Jews.

Imagine Esther's racing mind and pounding heart as she read this letter. Her response reflects her inner thoughts. She responds by reminding Mordecai of all of the reasons she cannot do as he commanded. If she goes before the king without being summoned, the death penalty will be thrust on her unless the king extends the golden scepter and welcomes her into his presence. However, she has not been summoned by him in some time. Esther would surely be an unwanted visitor in his court.

Mordecai doubles down on his command in his final letter to Esther. Although we are not sure of his commitment to the ways of God, he seems to know something of God's covenant with His people. Mordecai seems to know that God will not let them perish because He has promised to make them numerous and protect their lineage, so a Savior can one day be born from these chosen people (Genesis 12:2-3). It also seems Mordecai knows that those who do not stand with God stand against Him. He cautions Esther. God will keep His commands. He will save His people and destroy those who are against Him: *Esther, will you stand with God as one of His chosen people, or will you stand against Him? Perhaps you have become queen at this moment so that you may stand with God.*

It is probably not a coincidence that in the entire book, Esther is the only person who has two names: Esther, her Persian name, and Hadassah, her Jewish name. Esther must decide which identity she will embrace—the one of the empire or the one of God's kingdom. Who will she trust with her life? The king of Persia or the God of Israel?

Esther's reply reveals her choice. Though she is likely trembling in fear, Esther chooses to reveal her identity as a Jew and approach the king with a request he will most likely not entertain. Even if it costs her life. She says, "I will go to the king even if it is against the law. If I perish, I perish" (Esther 4:16).

Esther asks Mordecai to encourage all the Jews he can to fast for three days while she does the same with her attendants. Then, she will act. This is the closest we come to seeing God blatantly mentioned in this book. They will not eat or drink for three days in order to gain some outside help with the monumental task at hand.

Was their fast dedicated to God? Did they also pray? We do not know. But what we do know is Esther saw her role as mediator between God's people and the king as something she would not be able to do alone. She had won the lustful affection of the king, but now she needed his political favor. This was out of her hands. Her life was in the hands of an unseen, unnamed God.

Esther's remarkable bravery is yet an imperfect example of another who approached a King on behalf of God's covenant people: Jesus. In God's kingdom, everyone is condemned to death, not by edict, but by their own sin. God saw that His people could not overcome sin on their own. Being a gracious and merciful King, He did not sit back in His palace and drink to their demise. Instead, He sent His son, Jesus, to be the mediator. Jesus lived a perfectly sinless life, yet chose to willingly die on the cross to settle the debt between God and His people. Esther was reluctant, but Jesus was willing, even to the point of death on a cross. He bore the full wrath of God the Father so that all who believe in Him can be saved.

Esther's story teaches us that God will sometimes choose to use us as instruments in His redemptive plan for the world. We should consider where God has placed us and with courage, stand up for what is right. But we are not the heroes or heroines when we do this. God has providentially placed us where we are, He gives us the courage to act, and He controls every situation and outcome.

What a tremendous blessing to be invited into God's work in the world. However, even our refusal to participate cannot stop God's plans. His plans hinge on only one person: Jesus, our perfect hero and mediator. In Him, there is salvation and redemption for all who believe. And one day, He will return to rid the earth of sin and death forever. God's will cannot be thwarted.

God's will cannot be thwarted.

Read Romans 12:1. What similarities do you see between this verse and Esther's commitment to act?

God providentially presided over Esther's promotion to the position of queen, and He had indeed placed her there "for such a time as this." Where has God placed you? How do you think God intends to use you for His glory in these places?

What practical steps can you take to follow the example of Esther and the greater example of Jesus to give your life over to God's plans and purposes?

Slowly read and contemplate the hymn on the next page. Allow it to be a prayer from you to God.

take my life and let it b

FRANCES RIDLEY HAVERGAL, 1874

Take my life and let it be
consecrated, Lord, to thee.
Take my moments and my days;
let them flow in endless praise,
let them flow in endless praise.

Take my hands and let them move
at the impulse of thy love.
Take my feet and let them be
swift and beautiful for thee,
swift and beautiful for thee.

Take my voice and let me sing
always, only, for my King.
Take my lips and let them be
filled with messages from thee,
filled with messages from thee.

Take my silver and my gold;
not a mite would I withhold.
Take my intellect and use
every power as thou shalt choose,
every power as thou shalt choose.

Take my will and make it thine;
it shall be no longer mine.
Take my heart it is thine own;
it shall be thy royal throne,
it shall be thy royal throne.

Take my love; my Lord, I pour
at thy feet its treasure store.
Take myself, and I will be
ever, only, all for thee,
ever, only, all for thee.

The courage of esther

READ ESTHER 5:1-8

The day had come. It was time. Perhaps Esther looked through her attire options, her hands shaky as she pushed aside lovely, form-fitting dresses for something more sensible. She was not going to the king as a lover but as a queen interceding for her people. She chose her royal robes. Only three days earlier, she had learned about the impending genocide of her people and how her husband, the king, had signed off on it. Now, it was time to do something about it.

As she readied herself, maybe she rehearsed the plan in her head. Stay calm, take slow and steady steps, make eye contact with the king, then humbly wait to see his response. Perhaps she remembered Vashti and how her disobedience had caused banishment. And maybe she remembered Bigthan and Teresh—how the king wasted no time sending them to the gallows when they crossed him. Would she be given one of these same consequences? Only time would tell. Ready as she would ever be, she started the walk from her quarters to the royal courtroom.

Mordecai could not see the plan unfolding, but most likely, he waited, anxious and rest-less, at the gate of the citadel. What would be Esther's fate? What would be the fate of the Jews? Was this perhaps the reason Esther was chosen as queen? Could the God of Israel have been planning this all along?

Step, step, step. Heart pounding, shallow breaths, lip quivering. We can picture it in our minds. Esther entered the inner courtyard. One can imagine that the room, normally bustling with royal attendants, fell silent, all eyes wide and fixated on her. Surely everyone knew she had not been summoned. Would she receive the king's welcome or his wrath?

When the king's eyes found Esther's, he felt no displeasure. She had won his favor. But he did wonder what brought her into his presence. He knew she must have come for a reason. Certainly, she would not have risked her life just to say hello. He extended the royal scepter and invited Esther closer, asking her what it was she desired.

Maybe at this moment, Esther could feel the adrenaline begin to fade. Perhaps her focus shifted from her fears to the job she was there to do. This was not the right time or place to reveal her identity as a Jew and the fate of her people due to Haman's plans. She wanted to speak to the king in a more private setting. She invited the king and Haman to a banquet, which she had already prepared, a sign that some part of her expected to find the king's favor and sit with him at her banquet table.

The king and Haman set out at once for the banquet. While there, the king enjoyed a little wine and again asked Esther about her desires. He assured her, "Whatever you ask will be given to you. Whatever you want, even to half the kingdom, will be done" (Esther 5:6). For reasons we cannot know, Esther did not ask for the safety of the Jews at that moment either, but instead, she invited Haman and the king to another banquet the next day. We will see tomorrow that the time in between banquets will be providentially used by God, as has been the case for each and every moment thus far in the book of Esther.

But for today, let us look back at the moment Esther entered the view of the king. Esther had a plan. She risked her life on behalf of the covenant people of God. Haman also had a plan. He wanted to sacrifice the lives of many to exalt himself and his own agenda. Esther's plan was of the kingdom of God. Haman's plan was for the empire of man. We will find out if Esther's plan is successful soon. But first, we must look at her bravery and what it means for us today.

Esther's bravery was not her own but was from the Lord. 1 Peter 4:11 says, "If anyone speaks, let it be as one who speaks God's words; if anyone serves, let it be from the strength God provides, so that God may be glorified through Jesus Christ in everything." God strengthens us to do the work He has placed before us. Anything we do for Him is through His giving us the ability to do so. Esther was no exception. Bravery is God-given, and there will be times God asks us to be brave for His glory.

At every turn in this book, we are left asking—who is really in control here? As we read in Psalm 24:1, "The earth and everything in it, the world and its inhabitants, belong to the Lord." It seems it is not the ones who appear powerful who are in control. Rather, it is God who, though often unseen, is all-powerful over all things.

God strengthens us

TO DO THE WORK HE HAS PLACED BEFORE US.

Prior to chapter 5, Esther is only called Queen Esther once. She is called Queen Esther at least ten times between her moment of bravery before the king and the end of the book. Why do you think this is significant?

Read Romans 6:12-13. Haman planned for the unrighteous destruction of God's kingdom, while Esther planned for the righteous deliverance of God's people. Are there areas in which you are living as a weapon for unrighteousness?

Read Acts 4:13-20. What do you learn about bravery and boldness from this passage?

Read Psalm 24:1. What does this verse imply about God's sovereignty? How might meditating on this verse impact how you approach current hardships in your life?

haman plots mordecai's demise

READ ESTHER 5:9-14

Nothing reveals the heart quicker than emotions. If the heart is the thermostat, emotions are the climate the heart produces. From bitter cold to raging hot, what we feel shows in what we express and how we express it. In Esther 5:9, Haman is "full of joy and in good spirits," but it seems within mere moments he is "filled with rage." Interestingly, the same circumstance fueled both his joy and his rage: the recognition of his significance.

Having just departed an exclusive banquet with the king and queen, Haman's ego was stroked. Not just anyone would be invited to such an affair. His invitation proved his significance in the empire. But only moments later, as he passes the king's gate on his way home, he sees Mordecai. Mordecai does not stand or honor Haman in any way. Haman's sense of significance shatters. How could Mordecai do such a thing? Does Mordecai not know who he is?

But that is just the thing. Who is Haman? He is a man who has built a little empire of achievements within the man-made empire of Persia. He feels big, but truly, he is quite small. He just does not know it yet. And because he does not know how insignificant he is—or maybe, it is because deep down inside, he does know—he has become obsessed with maintaining his fragile self-significance. He has become obsessed with himself. What does the Bible tell us about this obsession?

Let us look at Romans 1:21-22, 25: "For though they knew God, they did not glorify him as God or show gratitude. Instead, their thinking became worthless, and their senseless hearts were darkened. Claiming to be wise, they became fools... They exchanged the truth of God for a lie, and worshiped and served what has been created instead of the Creator, who is praised forever. Amen."

Self-obsession leaves no room for glorifying the Creator. It is idolatry. Haman's joy and his rage both reflect what we already know about him: He hates God, His ways, and His people. And it is a warning to us. Our emotions can help us detect what we idolize. For example, we may feel joy when our idol is close but rage when it is taken away. Surely this is not to say we are guilty of idolatry every time we feel happy or angry, but it is something we learn to be aware of through Haman's story.

So, what does Haman do with his rage? He covers it up with self-exaltation. He gathers together his wife and his friends, and he tells them of his wealth, number of sons, honors, and rank. Do you think Haman's wife needed a reminder of how many sons she had birthed? Probably not.

Regardless, after listing all his many achievements, Haman said, "Still, none of this satisfies me since I see Mordecai the Jew sitting at the King's Gate all the time" (Esther 5:13). Haman's ego could not stand even one ounce of dishonor. He felt if he could rid the world of the one person who did not bow to him, then he would be satisfied. But the self can never be satisfied within itself. Haman was wrong.

His friends gave him the most terrible advice. They basically said, "You do you, Haman. If you hate the guy that much, just do whatever feels right." He listened to his friends and chose to seek vengeance on Mordecai. He decides to construct a 75-foot-high gallows, upon which he could impale Mordecai. The height, the timing, and the construction of the gallows are all absurd. Idolatry—especially drunken idolatry fueled by unrighteous friends—is just plain ridiculous.

Haman's callous plan to take Mordecai's life shows us that idolatry is the path to death. But there is another path, and it is the one that leads to life.

In Matthew 7:13-14, Jesus says, "Enter through the narrow gate. For the gate is wide and the road broad that leads to destruction, and there are many who go through it. How narrow is the gate and difficult the road that leads to life, and few find it." Then in John 14:6, Jesus says, "I am the way, the truth, and the life. No one comes to the Father except through me."

The path to life is not found in one's self but in Jesus. Haman's deep opposition to God would eventually be his undoing. And it will be no different for anyone else. There may be temporary joy, like Haman experienced in chasing after life's highs, but true significance, lasting joy, and eternal peace come only from Jesus.

All people were created by God and for God. As long as anyone lives by the rules of self and for themselves, they will not find peace. And even when we begin to seek after God, we realize that we have all sinned and fall short of the standards He calls acceptable (Romans 3:23). However, Jesus met all of God's standards. He lived a sinless life on earth and then gave His life as payment for the sins all men have committed.

Anyone who believes in Jesus has access to the Father and a life of abundant significance and joy. If only Haman had surrendered his pride to God, he might have experienced a different outcome. As we will see tomorrow, his outcome is grisly. But you can make the choice today to believe in Christ, be saved from your sin, and live a life at peace with God.

ALL PEOPLE WERE CREATED

by God and for God.

Read Proverbs 12:15. What steps could you take to seek wise counsel when difficult situations arise? List two to three godly people you could reach out to for wise counsel.

Read Philippians 2:3-4. List the things these verses tell us to do. Then, list the things they tell us not to do. How can you apply this to your life?

Haman wants attention from man, but as Christians, we know the person we are ultimately living to please is God. According to Isaiah 66:2, what kind of person does God acknowledge?

Write a prayer, asking God to help you avoid idolatry and center your life on Him and the salvation He provides through Jesus.

mordecai honored, haman humiliated

READ ESTHER 6, PHILIPPIANS 2:1-11

It is the night after Esther's first banquet with Haman and King Ahasuerus. Esther is presumably asleep, although, with the genocide of her people and her upcoming request of the king on her mind, she very well may have been restless. Haman is constructing a 75-foot pole, called a gallows, on which to impale Mordecai because he despises Mordecai for not honoring him. And King Ahasuerus is oblivious to all of this. After a lovely banquet with his queen and top adviser, he lay down to sleep.

Only, King Ahasuerus cannot sleep. No matter how hard he tries, rest evades him. So, he does what any of us would do—he finds something to entertain himself, asking for the daily records book to be read. Maybe this dull book had lulled him to sleep before, and he hoped it would help again. However, the entry read on this particular night was not at all dull. It was a recount of the way Mordecai saved the king from an assassination plot. The king had forgotten about this epic tale; after all, it happened almost five years ago.

The king asked what had been done to honor Mordecai. Persian kings were lavish rewarders of loyalty because rewarding someone for foiling an assassination plot assured someone else would be quick to ruin the next attempt. Surprisingly, nothing had been done. How could this have been overlooked? He must correct this. Keeping in line with what we know of him, the king does not make a plan to honor Mordecai alone but wants to speak to one of his advisers. And which adviser happens to be available at this very early morning hour? Haman.

Haman, perhaps, has been awake all night as well. Sawing, hammering, digging. His people were readying the gallows. What if the noise of Haman's gallows being built is what kept the king awake? We cannot know for certain, but either way, Haman is now anxiously awaiting entrance to the king's court to ask permission to kill Mordecai. And he certainly expects to be granted this request. It took little convincing to obtain permission to kill an entire people group; surely, the king would not bat an eye at just one person's death.

Before Haman can make his request, the king brings him in and asks, "What should be done for the man the king wants to honor?" Haman can think of no one more worthy of honor than himself, so he begins to detail the kind of honor he would most like to receive. Unshockingly, it revolves around being recognized publicly for his significance—parading around town in royal robes, on a royal horse, with someone heralding his greatness for all to hear. But Haman is not the one who will receive this honor. He will be the one to bestow this honor on Mordecai at the king's request. Haman's request goes unsaid altogether. Instead of taking Mordecai's life, he is forced to celebrate it.

Haman is humiliated. Mordecai is honored. This is the first moment in the story when we see a power shift. Up until now, it seemed all of the cards were stacked against the Jews, but this is not so anymore. Not long ago, Mordecai was walking the streets, wailing for his people, and wearing sackcloth. Now, he wears royal robes and is preceded by shouts of honor. Even Haman's wife and friends see it. God is acting on behalf of His people, and anyone who stands in the way will not stand for long.

This may be one of the most important moments in the story. Circumstances are changing. And who is changing them? Was it Esther? No, she was entirely unaware of the plan against Mordecai. Was it Mordecai who had foiled yet another assassination plot? No, he had no opportunity to do so. It was God. He providentially kept sleep from King Ahasuerus. He orchestrated the exact page to be read from the records. He prevented the king from honoring Mordecai years ago. He brought Haman to the court in the wee hours of the morning, and He made a fool of Haman and honored Mordecai. While the world sleeps, God works. God alone is in control. If the providence of God was ever out of focus or hard to grasp in this story, it is now abundantly clear. God can humble anyone at any time, and He will humble all those who have positioned themselves against Him.

If we want to know how to live lives that are humble before God in order to receive His honor, we need to look no further than the life of Jesus. Philippians 2:1-11 tells us that Jesus emptied Himself, took on the form of a servant, and humbly obeyed God, even to the point of death on a cross. In response, God exalted Him, and one day, every person will bow—in heaven and on earth and under the earth—and every tongue will confess that He is Lord. Of course, we are not God like Jesus is. Even though all those who believe will share in His glory and reign with Him in eternity, we will never hold such a high position as He. Still, Jesus's example of service and humility should be something we strive for, knowing God will honor those who walk in His ways and follow His commands.

In today's reading, we may be tempted to see ourselves as Mordecai, the overlooked one who is waiting on the hand of God for protection and honor. And your story may mirror Mordecai's in some ways. Yet perhaps we have more in common with Haman. We desire to be recognized and seen, and we will go to great lengths to rid our lives of anything that threatens our status. Today, we have a chance to realize we are not the ones worthy of honor, and our time is better spent honoring not ourselves but the Lord.

WHILE THE WORLD SLEEPS, GOD WORKS.

God alone is in control.

Reflect for a moment on your life. In what areas have you, like Haman, pursued honor for yourself? How could you instead honor God in that area?

What do Psalm 25:9 and Proverbs 16:5 tell you about God's heart toward the proud and the humble?

What would it look like to live out Philippians 2:1-11 in your life?

Write a prayer, praising Jesus for being worthy of honor.

the providence of God

Greek: πρόνοια *(pronoia)*

MEANS "FORETHOUGHT"

Providence is derived from the Latin word *providere* which means "to foresee."

GOD IS PROVIDENT OVER	the physical universe (matter, inanimate objects), animate beings (plants, animals), and rational beings (humans who uniquely possess free will)
GOD'S PROVIDENCE LEADS TO	the accomplishment of His will, the glorification of Himself, spiritual blessing, spiritual growth
GOD'S PROVIDENCE DOES NOT NECESSARILY LEAD TO	physical blessing, health, immediate happiness
GENERAL PROVIDENCE	God generally sustains the earth and its inhabitants through the laws of nature (e.g., gravity, water, light, and energy from the sun)
SPECIAL PROVIDENCE	God chooses certain people to fulfill special roles in His plan and purpose. He divinely leads and guides them to fulfill their unique purpose (e.g., Moses, Abraham, David, the disciples, Paul)

WEEK TWO — DAY FIVE

haman destroyed

READ ESTHER 7

Have you ever made a decision that you thought would be small and unnoticeable but ended up causing a major disruption? Maybe you told a small white lie to cover a mistake at work and ended up getting fired. Maybe you let a harmful word slip from your mouth, not realizing the devastation it would bring to the person with whom you were speaking. Most of us have experienced unexpected consequences of what we thought was a seemingly small decision. Haman did too.

Haman had been forced to honor Mordecai, whom he despised. Ironically, Haman had planned Mordecai's death that very day but ended up celebrating his life. After this embarrassing turn of events, he sulked home to pout. And then before he knew it, he was whisked off to his second banquet with King Ahasuerus and Queen Esther. The banquet went fine enough until the king asked his queen what the occasion was for the shared meal. He wondered if she would finally tell him what she wanted from him. She would.

Esther had been preparing for this moment for days now. One wonders if she had memorized her exact words to avoid fumbling over them in fear. Did she make eye contact with the king? Did he see the fear in her eyes? We cannot know. However, we can picture her communicating humbly and clearly. Her request, if it pleased the king, was to spare her and her people. She then explains that her people have been sold to "destruction, death, and extermination." Her words seem to be a purposeful reflection of the very edict Haman had written (Esther 3:13). The king cannot stay silent after learning this news. He must know—who would threaten his queen?

Maybe he thought another empire or ruler was threatening Esther. But he is about to learn the threat came from within his very palace. Esther reveals that the man threatening her is Haman, which also reveals her identity as a Jew. Surely, both the king and Haman remember the edict they enacted against the Jews. Haman most assuredly remembers, and he becomes terrified. He thought his spat with Mordecai and his hatred for God's people had been quickly dealt with through the edict. He assumed he was in control of the situation, but he was not.

The king is enraged and flees to the garden. Why he fled, we do not know. But there was one factor he surely had to consider: Once an edict had been signed, it could not be revoked.

King Ahasuerus had signed off on the annihilation of the Jews, and there was no changing it. What had he done to his queen? How could he undo it? While King Ahasuerus fled, Haman stayed with the queen. This was forbidden. No man who was not a eunuch was ever to be alone with a woman who belonged to the king. But Haman knew his only chance at receiving mercy lay in the hands of Queen Esther. He fell on the couch where she reclined, probably begging for his life, just as King Ahasuerus reentered the room. Haman was too close to the queen, and the king called him on this act.

Haman was apprehended and marched to the gallows, the very gallows he made for Mordecai. And it was there that Haman was killed. His pride, sin, hatred, and unrighteousness caught up with him when he least expected it. He had formed a plot to annihilate the Jews because Mordecai would not bow to him, yet he died because he fell before another Jew, Esther. Haman's own power was much smaller than he realized.

Esther 7 reveals two important things to us. The first is that while God is perfectly provident, He uses people as part of His plan. Esther's bravery was a tool God used to bring the plight of His people before the king. Surely, God could have saved His people in a thousand different ways, yet He chose this one. God's plans do not hinge on our participation in them, but what a generous gift it is to be able to exert courage for kingdom causes. If we lack courage or choose not to stand when we find ourselves in "such a time as this" (Esther 4:14), we are not ruining God's plan; His will is not dependent on us. But we are choosing not to accept His invitation, which certainly is not the choice He wants us to make. Esther chose to humbly reveal her request and her identity, and God blessed her bravery.

The second thing we learn is that earthly empires are hopelessly corrupt. It is such a shame Esther could not have convinced the king to spare the Jews simply by telling him that life is precious and genocide is wrong. He would not have cared. She had to make him see the annihilation of the Jews would affect him personally because it would include his wife. God, on the other hand, rules His kingdom quite differently. He only ever does what is right. He disperses justice perfectly. He avenges those who do wrong. And He graciously made a way for His wrath to be satisfied in Jesus Christ. Those in Christ need not fear when they approach Him. He knows best and will do what is right every time.

GOD COULD HAVE SAVED HIS PEOPLE IN A THOUSAND DIFFERENT WAYS,

yet He chose this one.

Read Colossians 2:13-15. Describe the reversal of power in these verses. How does the story of Esther point toward the work of Christ and the way He has "disarmed the rulers and authorities and disgraced them publicly"?

List two to three ways you see God working behind the scenes in today's reading. What does this tell you about the ways God may be working in your life?

Read 2 Timothy 2:13. Based on today's study and this verse, what is your role in the plan of God? What is God's role?

In your life, where are you standing courageously for God? Where are you not yet standing courageously? What do you think would happen if you chose to start being courageous in these areas?

THIS SAYING IS TRUSTWORTHY:
FOR IF WE DIED WITH HIM,
WE WILL ALSO LIVE WITH HIM;
IF WE ENDURE, WE WILL ALSO
REIGN WITH HIM; IF WE DENY HIM,
HE WILL ALSO DENY US; IF WE ARE
FAITHLESS, HE REMAINS FAITHFUL,
FOR HE CANNOT DENY HIMSELF.

2 Timothy 2:11-13

Week two reflection

REVIEW ESTHER 4-7

Paraphrase the passage from this week.

What did you observe from this week's text about God and His character?

What does this week's passage reveal about the condition of mankind and yourself?

How does this passage point to the gospel?

How should you respond to this passage? What specific action steps can you take this week to apply this passage?

Write a prayer in response to your study of God's Word. *Adore God for who He is, confess sins that He revealed in your own life, ask Him to empower you to walk in obedience, and pray for anyone who comes to mind as you study.*

WEEK THREE — DAY ONE

the new edict

READ ESTHER 8

The great reversal that began in chapter 6 with Haman honoring Mordecai and continued in chapter 7 with the king sending Haman to the gallows carries on into chapter 8. Not only is Haman now gone, but when considering who should replace Haman as his closest adviser, the king looks no further than Mordecai. Esther had finally revealed her identity as a Jew and made known to the king that Mordecai was her cousin and caretaker. Mordecai was probably fresh in the king's mind, for King Ahasuerus had just honored Mordecai for saving his life yesterday. Who better to be his closest adviser? No one in his eyes. King Ahasuerus gives Haman's significant estate to Esther and the signet ring to Mordecai. Everything that once belonged to Haman, the enemy of the Jews, now belongs to these two. No one could have predicted this outcome!

However, there is still one great issue left unresolved—the fate of the Jewish people. The king seems oblivious to this. Although Esther's request was to save her life and the lives of her people, the king has yet to address the second part of the request. So, Esther must be brave again and bring her request before the king another time. She falls at his feet and reminds him that her people are facing certain death. The king once again extends the royal scepter. He is compassionate toward Esther and will act on this request. The original edict cannot be revoked, but he tells Esther to write another edict containing whatever pleases her concerning the Jews and to sign it with his ring.

The scribes are summoned, perhaps the same ones who drafted the first edict, in a scene that mirrors the scene from chapter 3. But this time, the scribes take down the words of Mordecai rather than the words of Haman. The edict is written, translated, sealed with the signet ring, and sent by mounted couriers. It needed to travel fast enough to reach every corner of the kingdom before the arrival of the day Haman planned to destroy the Jews.

The new edict gave the Jews the right to defend and fight for themselves should anyone choose to attack them on the thirteenth day of the twelfth month. They were allowed to "destroy, kill, and annihilate every ethnic or provincial army hostile to them," and even more than that, they were given permission to wipe out the families of the armies and take all of their possessions. This was a tactic used to greatly dissuade any person from attacking the Jews. Who would risk the lives of their children? Mordecai probably hoped no one would.

The edict was received by every province, and in Susa where there once was confusion and mourning, there was now gladness, joy, and honor. All of the Jews celebrated that their lives had been spared by the proclamation of this new law. And even more than this, many who were not Jews claimed to be because they feared the Jewish people and their powerful God. Identifying as a Jew was a fearful thing earlier in King Ahasuerus's reign, but now, it was a desired status.

In Persia, God did for Esther, Mordecai, and all the Jews what He promises to do for all of His people through the Messiah in Isaiah 61. He comforted those who were mourning (all the Jews), giving them a crown of beauty (Esther) in the place of ashes. He gave them splendid clothes (Mordecai) instead of despair, and He sentenced to disaster those who stood against the Lord (Haman and anyone else who would seek to kill the Jews).

The book of Esther tells the story of the gospel: a people sentenced to death, a courageous mediator, a compassionate king, and the gift of life where death once seemed certain. But the truth of the gospel is even better than the story of Esther. When we consider the gospel, we see that we have all been condemned, not just to earthly death but to eternal death because of our sin. And while Esther and Mordecai both played a role as mediators for the Jewish people, Jesus is a perfect mediator between God and man. He was not powerless as Esther and Mordecai were at times. Rather, He had infinite power yet chose to yield it and submit Himself to death.

Jesus presented His request to spare the lives of His people before the King, His Father, not with words alone but with action. He knew the debt of sin must be paid, and He chose to pay it with His death on the cross. God accepted His life given as a payment for sin, and therefore, anyone who believes in Christ is free from the threat of eternal death!

We all receive this good news, not through a traveling edict but through the Word of God illuminated by the Spirit of God. Our response should be like the Jews throughout Persia—gladness, joy, honor, and celebration! We have been freed from the power of sin and death. Jesus has bought our freedom, God has accepted His payment, and our mourning has been turned to joy! If the truth of the gospel has lost its luster in your life, may the story of Esther be a wonderful invitation to see the gospel afresh.

We have been freed

FROM THE POWER OF SIN AND DEATH.

Read Genesis 12:2-3. This was God's promise to Abraham when He called Abraham to be the founding father of God's people, the Jews. How do you see this promise playing out in Esther 8?

Read Isaiah 61:1-3. How do you see this passage lived out in Esther's story? How do you see it lived out in your story?

Read John 19:11. What does this tell you about earthly authority? How does understanding this truth affect the way you live?

Write down three to five ways the gospel impacts you. Write a prayer of thankfulness for the truth of the gospel.

the enemies of the jews destroyed

READ ESTHER 9:1-19

In Esther chapter 8, we see a new edict written and proclaimed. In Esther chapter 9, we see the edict in action. Today's reading takes place on the thirteenth day of the twelfth month, the month of Adar. You may remember, this is the day Haman chose by chance by rolling the pur to annihilate the Jews. But this day looks much different than he planned. For one, Haman is no longer alive to witness it, and additionally, the second edict has allowed the Jews to forcefully defend themselves from their attackers.

On this day, not only do the Jews stand ready to fight back, but God stands with them. Verse 2 says that fear of the Jews fell on every nationality. Where do you think it fell from? It was surely from the providential hand of God that has controlled every moment of the story up until this point. Even more than that, every royal official, governor, and administrator aided the Jews. They all revered and feared Mordecai and his high position in the palace.

Still, many chose to rise against the Jews, and they were all killed. It is reported that in the fortress of Susa, 500 men were killed, including the ten sons of Haman. Around the kingdom, 75,000 men were killed. Why would the Jews kill so many people when they themselves had just been freed from the fear of death?

The answer is complex, but observing the facts will help us sort it out. First, the Jews did not initiate an attack on anyone but only drew their swords against people who were the aggressors against them first. The people who attacked them were not reasonable. They were motivated by an other-worldly hatred for God and His people. If the Jews did not destroy them, they would seek to destroy the Jews. One wonders if some of these people were descendants of Agag like Haman. Remember, in 1 Samuel 15, God commanded the Israelite King Saul and his army to destroy every Amalekite, including King Agag, yet he did not. Were the Jews now finishing this task? Perhaps.

In the Old Testament, there were times when God used His people to enact a holy war, a righteous judgment against entire people groups. Another example of this is seen when the Israelites attacked Canaan in Joshua 6. The Canaanites were excessively evil, sacrificing their children, treating women abhorrently, and committing many "detestable acts." The Bible tells us the wages of sin is death (Romans 6:23), and these people, like all of us, were sinners who deserved death. However, when the Israelites attacked Canaan, God did save one family: the family of Rahab the prostitute. Rahab showed faith in God when she hid the Israelite spies in Joshua 2, and therefore, God saved her. God is just and righteous in life and death.

In Esther, we can infer the Jews were treating the battle they engaged in as a holy war. They were fighting against those who were fighting against God, and they had to meet their aggressors at their level of aggression. It was to kill or be killed. Yet although they were permitted to kill women and children and plunder the homes of the attackers, they did not. Historically, when Israelites fought a holy war, they did not take anything from those they conquered. A holy war was not about personal gain but about the holiness of God.

We may also have questions about Esther's request to extend the edict an additional day within the boundaries of Susa and impale Haman's already dead sons on poles. Was she being purely vindictive? It is possible. We do not know her motives. But it is also possible she knew the attacks against the Jews were not yet over, and she simply wanted permission for the Jews to continue to defend themselves. Publicly displaying the deceased enemy was a common practice signaling victory in Persian culture. Gruesome as it was, the public impaling of Haman's sons was a victory shout for the Jews (Joshua 8:29, 10:26).

What can we learn from today's rather dark reading and study? Yesterday, we detailed how the story of Esther is the story of the gospel. But, even in the gospel story, there is a violent and deadly battle that will be fought long after the initial victory of the cross. All who believe in Christ are saved from eternal death, but we also live in a world where the powers of evil still have an impact on us. We are in a holy war, and we must fight back. We have an assurance of victory, a God who will not let us fail. But we are not excluded from fighting. Our fight is not with flesh and blood. We do not fight with our fists or swords. Our war is against principalities and rulers of this world. And we fight by putting on the whole armor of God and standing against every scheme of the enemy (Ephesians 6:10-19).

This fight will be won completely and totally one day by Jesus. He has come to the earth once, and He will come again. When He comes again, He will fight the last and final holy war against sin and evil, and He will be eternally victorious. Evil will be banished, and peace will reign.

War is not an easy topic to discuss, but it is a reality for every believer in Christ. We are in between days. We live as already victorious but not yet seeing total victory over our enemies. Still, our victory is assured, for God will support us, deliver us, and win the ultimate victory through Jesus Christ.

We have an assurance of victory,

A GOD WHO WILL NOT LET US FAIL.

Read Joshua 6:17-25. These verses detail a holy war against the city of Jericho. What do these verses tell us about the holy war in Esther 9:1-19?

Read Ephesians 6:10-12. With whom are Christians in a war?

Read Ephesians 6:13-18. In what ways are Christians spiritually equipped for battle?

How does today's study impact the way you live?

the feast of purim established

READ ESTHER 9:20-32

Can you remember back to the start of the book of Esther? The first chapter detailed an extravagant party serving to display the glory and honor of the Persian empire and King Ahasuerus. The party ended with the humiliation of the king when his queen at the time, Vashti, refused to come when he called her. In chapter 9, we are only one chapter from the end of the book of Esther, and another celebration is being announced. This time, though, the celebration is not in honor of the empire or the king but in honor of the deliverance of God's people and God's kingdom.

After the Jews defended themselves and prevailed against their enemies, they celebrated and feasted together. Even though the circumstances were still less than desirable and they were forced to retaliate against those who attacked them, they had been preserved in the face of danger. How sweet life must have seemed to those who feared it was going to be taken away from them. How thankful they must have been to still have breath in their lungs. They thought the day of reckoning would lead them to their graves, but here they were, rejoicing in the company of their loved ones, savoring a meal together, and celebrating the bright future that awaited them. Esther 9:22 says, "their sorrow was turned into rejoicing and their mourning to a holiday." Is this not the message of the gospel?

When Jesus died, His disciples mourned, hid in fear, and doubted if He really was the Messiah who had come to save them. For three days, they were bewildered. Had they been right to trust that Jesus was Lord? Had He left them when they needed Him the most? They received their answer three days later. Jesus had not left, and He had not abandoned them. His death paid the price for their sins and made a way for them to experience eternal life. The death of Jesus redeemed the lives of those who believed in Him. It took the disciples time to understand the death and resurrection of Jesus, but as their understanding grew, so did their joy in Christ!

Before Jesus died, He instituted the sacrament of communion (Luke 22:14-20). During His last meal with His disciples, He took a cup of wine and passed it around for each disciple to take a sip. He explained that the wine represented the new covenant of His blood which would be poured out for many. He also broke a piece of bread and explained it represented His body which would be beaten and broken. He told the disciples to continue this practice of breaking bread and drinking wine in remembrance of Him. He knew that men easily forget the things of God, even the greatest things, like salvation from sins. Jesus instituted a sacrament that could be regularly practiced to remind believers of the sacrifice of Jesus and its implications for those who believe. Unless we remind ourselves of God and His work in our lives, we can easily forget it.

Mordecai knew man's tendency to forget as well. Therefore, he sent letters to all the Jews in the Persian empire, ordering them to celebrate their relief from Haman and their enemies every year. This celebration was called the Feast of Purim. Even the name of the feast is ironic as it is named after the pur, or die, that Haman cast to decide the day of execution for the Jews. By the provident hand of God, that day ended up being a day of deliverance rather than a day of destruction. One component noticeably missing from the declaration of the Feast of Purim is the mention of God as the deliverer and the One being celebrated. As we know, this is not unusual in the book of Esther. But still, we can see deliverance ultimately came at the hand of God, whether the book mentions God's name or not. Throughout history, Jewish people have celebrated the Feast of Purim. In fact, it is still celebrated every year in mid-March by Jews around the world. It is traditional to read the book of Esther aloud, eat, drink, and celebrate during the feast.

Chapter 9 ends with an interesting twist. Just as the book begins and ends with a feast, it also begins and ends with a letter sent to all 127 provinces because of the actions of a woman. The first letter, inspired by Vashti, promoted the dominion of men over their wives and emphasized the power of the king and, therefore, the power of all men. The second letter sent at the hands of Esther emphasizes the peace and security of all Jewish people in the empire. King Ahasuerus wanted dominion over his empire and his wives, but did he ever really achieve this? In the end, we see clearly that he was never as powerful as he imagined he was. He was only a pawn in the hands of Almighty God.

The way the beginning of Esther's story reflects the end of the story is striking. Every attempt the king and Haman made to exalt themselves in Esther 1 and 2 is mirrored with the Lord exalting Himself and His people in Esther 8 and 9. You may have heard Proverbs 19:21 before. It says, "Many plans are in a person's heart, but the Lord's decree will prevail." This truth compels us to submit our plans to the Lord and receive His decrees, even when they counteract our own. May this encourage us to remember that the Lord is sovereign over all things at all times. The future belongs to the Lord alone, and in that truth, we find hope and rest, even when facing the most difficult of circumstances.

Unless we remind ourselves of God

AND HIS WORK IN OUR LIVES, WE CAN EASILY FORGET IT.

The Jews in Persia experienced the preservation of their lives after fearing they would die. Read Ephesians 2:1-10. In the columns below, write down every word or phrase associated with being "dead in your trespasses and sin" and "made alive with Christ."

DEAD IN YOUR TRESPASSES + SIN	MADE ALIVE IN CHRIST

Reflect on the columns above. Write a prayer of celebration and thanksgiving for what God has saved you from and what He has saved you to.

Take time to remember some other ways God has worked in your life. How have you seen God moving in your life in the past week? In the past six months? In the past five years?

Read Proverbs 19:21. Though we make many plans for our lives, God is ultimately in control. Make a list of circumstances or situations that you are trying to control in your life. Spend a few moments in prayer about each situation you list, submitting your plans to God's will.

the deliverance of God

Hebrew = יָשַׁע
Pronunciation = (yaw-shah')
Meaning = *delivered, rescued, safe*

In the Old Testament, God delivers His people from danger, fear, and suffering countless times. He sometimes uses people to accomplish His deliverance and sometimes directly takes action Himself. When God delivers His people, it leads to safety, security, and peace.

Every act of deliverance in the Old Testament is a foreshadowing of the ultimate deliverer, Jesus, who appears in the New Testament. Jesus delivers from death, judgment, and hell all who believe in Him. God's deliverance leads those who are saved to worship, trust, and obey Him.

GOD'S DELIVERANCE IN THE BIBLE

DELIVERER	DELIVERERED FROM	REFERENCE
Joseph	Famine	Genesis 41:56-57
Moses	Egyptian Slavery	Exodus 3:8, 18:10
Othniel	Conquest of King Cushan-rishathaim	Judges 3:8-10
Ehud	Eglon, King of Moab	Judges 3:12-30
David	The Philistines	2 Samuel 8:1
Jesus	Sin, Death, Evil, Judgment, Hell	Luke 4:18, 1 Thessalonians 1:10

waiting for a better deliverer

READ ESTHER 10:1-3

When was the last time you enjoyed uninterrupted rest and relaxation? Was it a vacation to a faraway place? A long weekend at home spent with people you love? Oh, what a joy times of retreat are, but no matter how sweet they are, they cannot last forever. Eventually, they end, and we are thrown into the demands of daily life once again. Esther 10:1-3 probably felt a bit like this for the Jews. One day they are rejoicing, feasting, and celebrating, and the next they are slapped with a heavy tax by King Ahasuerus.

You may remember the king freed the provinces from tax payments in Esther 2:18 in order to celebrate Esther's crowning as queen. Here, several years later, he reinstates them. Ancient taxes were not the same as taxes today. We know from historical records that empires like Persia relied on their provinces to supply everything they needed for military conquests, the development of the empire's infrastructure, and the needs of those within the royal citadel. Often, a province would be assigned a period of time, maybe one month or maybe four months, during which they were called upon to provide whatever the empire needed. The empire may ask for money, food, or even labor. These demands were placed on the provinces without regard for their ability to pay them. Empiric taxes often meant the residents of the taxed provinces could barely provide for their own people.

In light of this, we understand the weight of King Ahasuerus's announcement of the return of taxation. It meant daily life would be a struggle. It meant the Persian people, including Persian Jews, would work dutifully day after day, only to have much of what they worked for taken from them. And ultimately, it meant that although the Jews experienced a temporary victory, they were still awaiting true freedom and everlasting joy.

In Esther 10:2-3, we learn Mordecai has increased in fame and honor. He pursued prosperity and well-being for all Jews, and he did this from a very influential place in the king's court. Yet, he was second in command. The irrational, angry, compulsive King Ahasuerus was still in power. We know God is sovereign over the king and uses all he says and does for His own plans and purposes. So, why did God allow King Ahasuerus to rule in such a harsh way? We cannot know for certain. But the last three verses of Esther remind us that even when we experience temporary victory in our lives, there will always be pain and hardship until the final victory of Christ at His second coming.

Esther and Mordecai were brave and strong leaders who played a part in the deliverance of their people. But their deliverance was not complete. They could not save God's people from the effects of sin. Sin condemns all people before God. It renders us unworthy to be in a relationship with Him. And sin's effects are not only felt between God and man but also from man to man. One person's sin can cause deep pain to another person. These verses remind us that the brokenness of the world was still pervasive, even after the deliverance of the Jews from the plans of Haman.

This truth makes us long for a better deliverer—a deliverer who can solve the problem of sin once and for all. It makes us long for Jesus. When Jesus arrived almost 500 years later, He was the Redeemer for whom the Persian Jews truly longed. He loved, served, healed, restored, and confronted all sin and evil for three years in His earthly ministry. Then, He gave His life as payment for all sins for all time through His death on a cross. But, remarkably, death was not the end for Him. He rose again to life, proclaiming victory over death forever. Not only this, but Jesus invites all of humanity to believe in Him as the Savior for our sin. As a result, we can experience eternal life, joy, and freedom in Him—what the Persian Jews desired, Jesus is for all mankind. He is the better deliverer.

Those who believe in Jesus have eternal victory over sin and death, but we still deal with the daily fallout of a world full of sin. We are still awaiting the redemption of the whole earth, which the Bible says will take place at the second coming of Christ. When He comes, He will wage war against sin and evil, and He will win. Then, there will be a new heaven and a new earth where God will dwell with His people. Revelation 21:5 says of this new heaven and earth, "Then the one seated on the throne said, 'Look, I am making everything new.'"

The Persian Jews experienced deliverance, but they could not escape the empire completely. However, all those who are in Christ will one day be a part of a new, glorious kingdom ruled by goodness, justice, peace, and love. We all long for a life like this. We were made to long for a life like this. And all those who believe will experience this kind of eternal life in God's kingdom forevermore.

Jesus is for all mankind.

HE IS THE BETTER DELIVERER.

Is this how you expected the book of Esther to end? Why do you think the author chose to include chapter 10 rather than concluding on a higher note with chapter 9?

How have you felt the effects of your sin and the sin of others in your life? When will believers cease to feel the effects of sin?

Read Psalm 40:1-5. How is the Lord described in this passage as our deliverer?

Write a prayer, expressing your desire for Jesus to return to earth soon.

READ GALATIANS 4:4-5, ROMANS 12:1, REVELATION 11:15, ROMANS 8:28, JOHN 3:16

Through this study, we have dived deeply into the ancient Persian world and the lives of King Ahasuerus, Queen Esther, Haman, and Mordecai. As we wrap up our study of this dynamic book of the Bible, let us review the themes we watched unfold and consider how they will impact our lives moving forward.

DIVINE PROVIDENCE – GALATIANS 4:4-5

Long before there was an imminent threat against the Jews in Persia, God was orchestrating a plan to rescue them. While many Jews left Persia to resettle in Jerusalem, Mordecai and Esther's relatives stayed in Susa. Mordecai worked within the citadel in service to the empire. Esther was given extraordinary beauty and favor from birth. God orchestrated all of these details for the accomplishment of His plan to not only save the Persian Jews but to preserve the family line from which the Messiah would be born.

Galatians 4:4-5 describes the birth of Jesus: "When the time came to completion, God sent his Son, born of a woman, born under the law, to redeem those under the law, so that we might receive adoption as sons." God's plan all along was to save men from their sin and eternal death through Jesus. For that plan to come to pass, He needed to preserve the Jews from whom Jesus would come. God's plans always come to pass. He providently guides and directs them through time and trials. God's providence reminds us of His surpassing power, which leads us to trust Him in all things.

HUMAN BRAVERY – ROMANS 12:1

Esther's moment of bravery before the king did not happen of her own willpower. In fact, we learned it took quite a bit of convincing. Yet, when she acted in bravery, God granted her favor, and her courage saved countless lives. We should consider where in our own lives God is asking us to stand for Him with courage and bravery. Esther's story encourages us to believe God has providently placed us where we are, so we can advance His kingdom there. Bravery is not always about big moves and brazen actions. Sometimes, it is about standing in obedience in the strength of God.

THE PERISHING EMPIRES OF MEN AND THE IMPERISHABLE KINGDOM OF GOD – REVELATION 11:15

Esther's story brought attention to the struggle all God's people face living under the empires of the world. The world's rulers are often evil, malicious, and sinful while God is good, just, and gracious. The world's empires and God's kingdom are always at odds with one another. Yet empires of men can never jeopardize or destroy the kingdom of God. God is in control of all empires and uses them for His kingdom. One day, the earth will be free from evil empires, and God's kingdom will stand victorious. Revelation 11:15 describes that moment: "The kingdom of the world has become the kingdom of our Lord and of his Christ, and He will reign forever and ever." This truth gives us hope that no matter what trials we endure, our future is secure in God's imperishable kingdom.

GOD'S RESPONSE TO HUMAN EVIL – ROMANS 8:28

Human evil and corruption abound in Esther's story. Haman was the chief example, although King Ahasuerus is certainly not a model of goodness either. Our study of God's response to human evil revealed that God executes justice, both on earth and in eternity. Not everyone experiences just consequences for their wrongs on earth, but in eternity, everyone will unless freed from their guilt by salvation in Jesus.

God is also sovereign over evil. Evil cannot occur unless God allows it, which brings us to our third revelation of how God handles evil. He uses the evil He allows for His glory and the good of His people. He does not completely eradicate evil in the book of Esther or in our own lives. He will do that one day when Jesus returns to establish a new heaven and new earth. But for now, He sovereignly presides over it, working through it to accomplish His perfect plan.

FORESHADOWING THE GOSPEL – JOHN 3:16

Esther displayed for us a dramatic rescuing of God's people from the threat of death. What is that, if not the message of the gospel? Death to life. Condemnation to salvation. Ostracized to accepted. The Persian Jews faced physical death at the decree of Haman, but all people face spiritual death due to the decree of God. Perfection is the requirement to receive forgiveness from sins and experience eternal life with God, and no person can fulfill that requirement on their own.

God placed Esther and Mordecai in a position of authority, allowing them to act as mediators before the king on behalf of the people. Similarly, God placed Jesus in a place of authority, allowing Him to mediate on behalf of all sinful men before God. Jesus gave His life on the

cross to pay the price of sin once for all. God accepted His sacrifice and grants life evermore to all who believe in Jesus. Jesus offers us the chance to move from condemnation to salvation, from death to life, from being ostracized from God to being brought near. All of Esther is a beautifully illustrated foreshadowing of the gospel.

As we come to the end of this study, may we consider how the book of Esther has impacted us. Perhaps we learned something new about these biblical figures. Maybe our eyes were opened to understand God's providence in the world. Hopefully, our faith has been bolstered to believe God is at work in our lives, even when we cannot clearly see it. God is a God of providence and deliverance. He is trustworthy and true. He is a secure place to put our faith and hope. There is no one like Him and no one who can compare to Him. If we have learned anything from the book of Esther, we have learned to rest in who He is, even when we cannot see what He is doing.

God is at work in our lives,

EVEN WHEN WE CANNOT CLEARLY SEE IT.

Which of the themes in Esther most impacted you? How will it change the way you live moving forward?

Read Hebrews 13:14. What has Esther taught you about how to live faithfully for the kingdom of God while living in the empire of the world?

What human evil have you experienced in your life? In what ways have you also experienced God's sovereignty and redemption of evil?

Write a prayer asking God to reveal how He is asking you to be courageous for Him in the places He has called you.

THE SEVENTH ANGEL BLEW HIS TRUMPET, AND THERE WERE LOUD VOICES IN HEAVEN SAYING, THE KINGDOM OF THE WORLD HAS BECOME THE KINGDOM OF OUR LORD AND OF HIS CHRIST, AND HE WILL REIGN FOREVER AND EVER.

revelation 11:15

Week three reflection

REVIEW ESTHER 8-10

Paraphrase the passage from this week.

What did you observe from this week's text about God and His character?

What does this week's passage reveal about the condition of mankind and yourself?

How does this passage point to the gospel?

How should you respond to this passage? What specific action steps can you take this week to apply this passage?

Write a prayer in response to your study of God's Word. *Adore God for who He is, confess sins that He revealed in your own life, ask Him to empower you to walk in obedience, and pray for anyone who comes to mind as you study.*

GOD IS A GOD OF

providence and deliverance.

what is the gospel?

THANK YOU FOR READING AND ENJOYING THIS STUDY WITH US! WE ARE ABUNDANTLY GRATEFUL FOR THE WORD OF GOD, THE INSTRUCTION WE GLEAN FROM IT, AND THE EVER-GROWING UNDERSTANDING IT PROVIDES FOR US OF GOD'S CHARACTER. WE ARE ALSO THANKFUL THAT SCRIPTURE CONTINUALLY POINTS TO ONE THING IN INNUMERABLE WAYS: THE GOSPEL.

We remember our brokenness when we read about the fall of Adam and Eve in the garden of Eden (Genesis 3), where sin entered into a perfect world and maimed it. We remember the necessity that something innocent must die to pay for our sin when we read about the atoning sacrifices in the Old Testament. We read that we have all sinned and fallen short of the glory of God (Romans 3:23) and that the penalty for our brokenness, the wages of our sin, is death (Romans 6:23). We all need grace and mercy, but most importantly, we all need a Savior.

We consider the goodness of God when we realize that He did not plan to leave us in this dire state. We see His promise to buy us back from the clutches of sin and death in Genesis 3:15. And we see that promise accomplished with Jesus Christ on the cross. Jesus Christ knew no sin yet became sin so that we might become righteous through His sacrifice (2 Corinthians 5:21). Jesus was tempted in every way that we are and lived sinlessly. He was reviled yet still yielded Himself for our sake, that we may have life abundant in Him. Jesus lived the perfect life that we could not live and died the death that we deserved.

The gospel is profound yet simple. There are many mysteries in it that we will never understand this side of heaven, but there is still overwhelming weight to its implications in this life. The gospel tells of our sinfulness and God's goodness and a gracious gift that compels a response. We are saved by grace through faith, which means that we rest with faith in the grace that Jesus Christ displayed on the cross (Ephesians 2:8-9). We cannot save ourselves from our brokenness or do any amount of good works to merit God's favor. Still, we can have faith that what Jesus accomplished in His death, burial, and resurrection was more than enough for our salvation and our eternal delight. When we accept God, we are commanded to die to ourselves and our sinful desires and live a life worthy of the calling we have received (Ephesians 4:1). The gospel compels us to be sanctified, and in so doing, we are conformed to the likeness of Christ Himself. This is hope. This is redemption. This is the gospel.

SCRIPTURES TO REFERENCE:

GENESIS 3:15	*I will put hostility between you and the woman, and between your offspring and her offspring. He will strike your head, and you will strike his heel.*
ROMANS 3:23	*For all have sinned and fall short of the glory of God.*
ROMANS 6:23	*For the wages of sin is death, but the gift of God is eternal life in Christ Jesus our Lord.*
2 CORINTHIANS 5:21	*He made the one who did not know sin to be sin for us, so that in him we might become the righteousness of God.*
EPHESIANS 2:8-9	*For you are saved by grace through faith, and this is not from yourselves; it is God's gift—not from works, so that no one can boast.*
EPHESIANS 4:1-3	*Therefore I, the prisoner in the Lord, urge you to walk worthy of the calling you have received, with all humility and gentleness, with patience, bearing with one another in love, making every effort to keep the unity of the Spirit through the bond of peace.*

Thank you for studying
God's Word with us

CONNECT WITH US
@thedailygraceco
@dailygracepodcast

CONTACT US
info@thedailygraceco.com

SHARE
#thedailygraceco

VISIT US ONLINE
www.thedailygraceco.com

MORE DAILY GRACE
The Daily Grace App
Daily Grace Podcast